D0075731

Public Virtue

Notre Dame Studies in Law and Contemporary Issues

Volume Two

Volume One
Nazis in Skokie:
Freedom, Community, and the First Amendment
Donald Alexander Downs

The University of Notre Dame Press gratefully acknowledges the generous support of The Honorable James J. Clynes, Jr., of Ithaca, New York, in the publication of titles in this series.

PUBLIC VIRTUE

Law and the
Social Character of Religion

Christopher F. Mooney, S.J.

University of Notre Dame Press
Notre Dame, Indiana

Library of Congress Cataloging in Publication Data

Mooney, Christopher F.
    Public virtue.

    (Notre Dame studies in law and contemporary issues ; v. 2)
    Bibliography: p.
    Includes index.
    1. Church and state—United States. 2. Christianity and law.
3. Sociology, Christian—United States. 4. Social ethics.
5. United States—Religion—1945-   . I. Title. II. Series.
BR516.M598   1986   291.1'77'0973   85-41014
ISBN 0-268-01561-9

Manufactured in the United States of America

To Margaret A. Farley, R.S.M.
Friend, Scholar, Woman of the Church

Contents

Biographical Note

Christopher F. Mooney, S.J., a member of the Pennsylvania Bar, is Academic Vice President of Fairfield University. He previously served as Chair of the Theology Department at Fordham University, President of Woodstock College, and Assistant Dean at the University of Pennsylvania Law School. He holds doctorates in both theology and law, and in recent years has had as his major interest the interface between religious and legal values. He has written five other books: *Teilhard de Chardin and the Mystery of Christ* (1966), which won the National Catholic Book Award, *The Making of Man* (1971), *Man Without Tears* (1975), *Religion and the American Dream* (1977), and *Inequality and the American Conscience* (1982).

Preface

The central theme of this volume is that American biblical religion has, and ought to have, an outward as well as an inward focus. Not only is it concerned vertically with the relationship of individual to God and with the inner spiritual life of religious communities; it is also concerned horizontally with the way in which our religious convictions relate to the secular human project and provide a prophetic critique of our national life. This horizontal concern has always been operative in America, and our culture, as historian Henry F. May has shown, owes much of its vigor and complexity to the great historical dialogue between secular and religious thought.[1] Such an outward focus necessarily brings religion into contact with law and politics, an interaction that has occasioned much comment in recent years, chiefly because it raises so many larger issues of public morality and social justice.[2]

These larger issues in turn pose two central questions which form a backdrop for the chapters that follow. First, when a particular religious group or one of its members enters the public sphere, are they seeking to promote only sectarian values or rather striving to understand these values in relation to the religious and nonreligious convictions of others? Second, when law and politics interact with such values, how will they go about separating these values from their narrow sectarian source so that their public scrutiny will secure benefits for the entire body politic? Both these questions reflect that perennial devotion to the common good which the Founders called "public virtue" (about which more in chapter one). This they expected all citizens to practice, to some degree at least, whether they were religiously motivated or not, and the government structured by the Founders was based upon this expectation. As we shall see, if they were to examine such public virtue today, they would have reason to be both satisfied and sad.

The issues I explore in these pages are not necessarily the most important, or even those where religion can be most decisive. The nuclear arms race, for example, surely poses the most urgent moral question now facing humankind. But its complexity almost demands book-length discussion, as the large number of recent studies testifies.[3] Racial inequality and prejudice constitute another dilemma that is truly moral and properly public, and one to which all religious traditions in America have spoken eloquently in recent years, not least through the religious appeals of Martin Luther King, Jr. I have, however, already devoted considerable space to the legal and the moral remedies for this phenomenon.[4] The issues I deal with in this volume are also inherently public in character and can be resolved only by appealing to our common national conscience. I believe that to speak to such issues, which by their nature will elicit more than a single moral or legal response, is precisely the public task of religion.

Chapter one speaks to the phenomenon of religion's continuing influence upon American public life, symbolized by the Presidential election of 1984. I argue that such influence is proper to the extent that it constitutes an exercise of "public virtue," that is to say, to the extent that it highlights the dangers of a shallow procedural democracy and acts as a catalyst for wide-ranging discussion of substantive questions of social justice and community good. Religion's task in this public sphere is to reverse the ever present tendency of citizens in an economically prosperous democracy to privatize their lives by immersing themselves exclusively in commercial pursuits. Through its own exercise of public virtue, religion seeks thus to promote the political and social involvement of all citizens, to some extent at least, in the larger interests of the public weal.

In chapter two the focus shifts from the role of religion for public life to the role of law for religion. There I seek to clarify the church-state relationship in America, as this has been established through the religion clauses of the First Amendment, and as it has been articulated historically and contemporarily through decisions by the United States Supreme Court. In one sense these clauses are simply a consequence of that ever-present involvement of religion in the public sphere that I discuss in chapter one. They are the legal ways we have devised to keep these two most important institutions separate, yet at the same time functioning together with a minimum of strife. For we believe as a nation that neither can fare well without the health of the other, and that it is precisely through law that our commitment to religious pluralism and freedom is concretized.

Morality and law intersect each other in chapter three, where the issue of law as a standard for public morality raises subsidiary questions of the range of such a standard, as well as its necessity and completeness. Law emerges here as a medium through which highly emotional public issues can be adjudicated under the guidance of careful argument. The key consequence of this is the urgent need for dialogue between lawyers and ethicists. Morality and public policy may be related, insofar as laws are shaped by the ethical beliefs of policy makers. But the two are also clearly distinct, since not every ethical value promotes the common good, and only those that clearly do can be the proper objects of legislation.

I am concerned in chapter four with one of the most influential institutions in the nation: the legal profession. With no single culture or single religious faith to bind them, Americans have found their communality to a large degree in the law. For it is law that finally protects them from one another and from government, and vindicates their rights when these are threatened. But because law has gradually separated itself from its original moral and religious foundation, its privatizing impulse has tended to become dominant and it no longer conceives its primary mission to be the responsible exercise of public virtue. Hence any individual aspiring to exercise such virtue as a lawyer will be able to avoid disillusionment only by retrieving from tradition the experience of law as vocation, that is, as a "calling" to public responsibility for the common good.

A more complex phenomenon is the subject of chapter five: the inherent risk in invoking the moral consensus of a nation to achieve ends that are narrowly political. Even though my narrative here deals with the public outrage that followed the sinking of the passenger liner *Lusitania* by a German submarine in the First World War, the reader will immediately recognize parallels with the 1983 downing by a Russian fighter of Korean Airlines Flight 007.[5] In the case of the *Lusitania*, however, we now know that public opinion was radically uninformed, that government concealment on matters of international law was deliberate, and that the religious self-righteousness of President

Wilson blinded him to moral realities. The fact that the event and its aftermath produced diplomatic repercussions which were at the time momentous, should urge extreme caution upon us today.

Finally, chapter six presents a case study: a particular religious group, the Roman Catholic Church, teaches in the public sphere matters of universal morality which it proposes as obligatory for all persons, whether Catholic or not. It maintains that the warrant for such teaching is not its own religious faith, but a universal natural moral law, which is in principle available to all and so open to public scrutiny. What must be recognized, however, is that it is always the medieval concept of natural law which is appealed to in such Roman Catholic analyses of the common good. The question for public scrutiny, then, is how precisely the moral argument is drawn from this medieval understanding of natural law. Methodology will be of great moment here, not only for credibility with society as a whole but also for the persuasiveness of the morality taught.

Four of these chapters have appeared earlier in journals, though each has been rethought and rewritten for the present volume.[6] I want to thank the editors of these journals for permission to unite these copyrighted materials together under their common theme. I must also express my gratitude to the editor of the University of Notre Dame Press, Richard Allen, whose continued encouragement and interest in this project helped both to sustain it and to bring it to completion.

A number of persons have read various chapters in their original form, and I am indebted to each, but especially to Margaret A. Farley, R.S.M., Gilbert L. Stark Professor of Ethics at Yale University Divinity School, who offered invaluable suggestions and criticism for the entire manuscript. Helen Zeccola carefully proofread the whole text, which was typed by Teresa Delco and Anne Baig with their usual accuracy; to each I express my sincere gratitude. And to Cecilia and Richard Mooney goes my warmest appreciation for their support over many years.

I

Religion in
The Public Sphere

To the surprise of many, the influence of religion upon public life in America continues to be strong, and has even intensified in recent years. This is contrary to a widespread assumption that religion has been playing a progressively diminishing role in modern American society. Such an assumption is usually based upon the phenomenon of "secularization," defined by Peter Berger as that "process by which sectors of society and culture are removed from the domination of religious institutions."[1] This process has indeed been one of the central facts of modern history, because through its impact the historical link that existed for centuries between church and state was finally broken. The result has been that church and state henceforth developed as separate sectors of society, that disestablishment became a synonym for secularization, and that religious pluralism was its cognitive corollary. In other words, religion in any given culture was no longer the "sacred canopy," to use Berger's term, the legitimator of the status quo, investing the existing social order with sacred meaning.

But this change, momentous as it has been, of itself says nothing at all about the erosion of religious influence or the demise of religious institutions. It says simply that the power relationships between church and state have shifted, and that their dominant roles are no longer necessarily compatible. Religious institutions are now free to exercise a critical function vis-a-vis government, something that has inevitably produced tensions between the two which in former times would have been muted or totally repressed.[2] The Presidential campaign of 1984 offered clear proof that religion has been neither totally privatized nor depoliticized, but is able to function easily and openly in the public sphere. Whether such functioning in 1984 was indeed healthy, either for church or state, is a question we shall address later in this chapter. To put this question in historical perspective, however, we must first examine two key phenomena of our national life, that of the "public church" and its impact on secular society, and that of "public virtue" and its influence upon the meaning of citizenship.

I

"Religion," say the authors of a recent sociological study, "is one of the most important of the many ways in which Americans 'get involved' in the life of their community and society. Americans give more money and donate more time to religious bodies and religiously associated organizations than to all other voluntary associations put together. Some 40 percent of Americans attend religious services at least once a week (a much greater number than would be found in Western Europe or even Canada) and religious membership is around 60 percent of the total population."[3] While the majority of Americans today have no difficulty accepting the doctrine of church-state separation, they nevertheless believe that religion ought to play a crucial role in the public sphere, that God calls them to be citizens as well as believers, that public life can have a truly religious significance, and that passionate faith commitment does not rule out critical patriotism and responsible citizenship.

Such Americans constitute what Martin Marty has called the "public church." This "public church," says Marty, is made up of the religious center of America—the mainline Protestant churches, the Roman Catholic church, and significant sectors of the evangelical and sectarian churches. Marty's focus here is limited to Christianity in America, but for my purposes in this chapter I would have to include also important segments of the Jewish community. This public church is characterized by a willingness to dialogue in public whenever questions are raised of social responsibility or the common good. It respects the beliefs of those of other religions or of no religion, and resists both the fundamentalist impulse that seeks only to make one's own religious beliefs prevail in public, as well as that individualistic impulse that views religion in any form as a purely private affair.[4]

Such convictions of the public church regarding the social impact of religion have a threefold basis. The first is the historical willingness of American churches to exercise a critical function in society. Before secularization, with establishment a key religious fact in society, churches rarely thought of their prophetic role to identify social problems or to press social grievances. Yet, as carriers of cultural and moral values, they did believe they had a duty to react when these values conflicted with those of society's status quo, and to press at times for change in the social order. When this happened, religious bodies activated that potential which is always theirs to confer legitimacy on some phenomenon or cause, a potential which can still be decisive even in the most secularized society.

Churches thus face toward both the private and the public spheres. They give a measure of stability to the former by explaining for their members the meaning of life and transcendence, as well as by providing them with personal identity and belonging in the community. In the public sphere, on the other hand, churches act as agents for transmitting (not uncritically) the operative values of society, formulating the moral aspects of political questions and seeking to interpret the biblical message for today's world. This effort to search out ways in which religious faith may have public policy implications has engaged religious people in what has come to be called "public theology," namely the articulation of a socially significant meaning of a particular tradition or a particular set of religious symbols. The moral vision of a just society, expressed in these symbols and traditions, can indeed be distinguished from the secular norms of public policy. But just as society and state are increasingly interpenetrating each other, so must any religious vision that is prevalent in the land inevitably weave itself into the fabric of political life.[5]

Such interpenetration has two obvious dangers. The first is that a particular religious institution will, in pressing its own theologically normative judgments, neglect to express these judgments also in that language and argument appropriate to civic discourse, independent of its own symbol system. Whenever this happens, an invaluable opportunity is lost to seek common ground with other religious groups, based upon a public morality and jurisprudence. This then tends to stimulate not consensus but sectarian conflict, because, as John Coleman has argued, no church can expect its own theological self-understanding to become public property enshrined by law. It can garner general support for the freedom it demands for its own religious convictions only if it bases its case simultaneously on secular argument.[6]

The second danger is the very opposite of the first, namely that government may in some measure try to restrict the freedom of churches to speak and act in the public sphere. Pressures to do so tend to originate in the belief that the religion clauses of the First Amendment should not only keep government from interfering with churches but also churches from interfering with government. This is in effect to claim that the exercise of religion ought to have no public face at all, but should be restricted to worship and religious instruction. Section 501 (c) (3) of the Internal Revenue Code, for example, now threatens churches with loss of tax exemption for "substantial" efforts to influence legislation. The effect of these restrictions, whose constitutionality is still to be decided by the Supreme Court, is inevitably to chill the freedoms of religion, speech, and petition, whereby churches have been empowered to intervene in the public realm whenever this is necessary to accomplish their religious and social mission.[7]

Besides the historical willingness of American churches to exercise a critical function in society, there is a second and more fundamental basis for the social impact of religion in America. This is the unabated vigor of the phenomenon known as "civil religion." I have written at some length on this subject elsewhere.[8] Suffice it to say here that this phenomenon represents a dynamic of religion as such in our society, quite distinct from any given religious institution, a dynamic that renders the social milieu of the United States historically, and perhaps irreversibly, religious. Historically, because the origin of the phenomenon was the conviction of the Founders that God was responsible for our nation's beginning, leading us as a chosen people, like Israel during the Exodus. And perhaps irreversibly, because through two centuries of domestic crises and international conflicts this belief has continued to thrive, rooted in the biblical covenant theology that says God will favor our undertakings as a nation if we keep his commandments, and will judge and punish us (as Lincoln insisted God was doing through the Civil War) if we are unfaithful to our destiny. Although unconnected with the teachings of any particular church (but not competing with any), this essentially religious dimension of our national experience provides many Americans even today (despite past and potential future misuse) with that religious legitimacy which they still want for their country. It also tends to foster in the individual citizen genuine public concern and participation, to deprivatize religious experience generally, and to diminish divisive sectarianism.

The continued significance of civil religion as an accepted phenomenon is a clear indication that religious and moral norms are of themselves neither alien nor sectarian in American life. They are simply part of our public sphere. Over the years they have mediated between the highly individualistic secular ideals of liberty and equality on the one hand, and that strong communitarian sense traditionally fostered by institutional religion on the other hand. Inevitably this amalgam of aspirations and convictions has affected many formal procedures in our political life. The "public theology" I mentioned earlier, precisely because it makes explicit use, in its commentary on the public scene, of ethical teachings, behavior paradigms, and morally revelatory events of the Bible, finds a natural resonance with these more secularized convictions of civil religion. Indeed, in language and concern it is sometimes difficult to tell them apart, a fact which has led John Coleman to argue that the distinctive and positive contribution of Christianity to citizenship lies in that concern for the public good which is ultimately the objective of both.[9] Public theology is keenly aware, for example, that politics is in some sense a moral enterprise, since politicians continually ask what is good and bad for society. Hence all their accommodations and compromises somehow become also moral judgments. Thus public theology not only responds to the moral questions of society but also contributes to the shaping of these questions. It not only analyzes moral dilemmas, it also helps to alleviate them.

Convictions of the public church regarding the social impact of religion are based, finally, on religion's power to orient toward the public sphere those highly individualistic searches for meaning and self-fulfillment which have come to characterize much of contemporary life.[10] Such searches often rely upon experiences of God and things spiritual which take little account of the traditional authority of churches. Yet because religious individualism of this type is basically biblical in its inspiration, and so tends to move not from authority to anarchy but from authority to conscience, it is frequently possible to reach it by appeal to the Bible's social dimension. For in both the Hebrew and Christian scriptures God's transcendence and majesty are inextricably linked to justice in society; God promises that a sinful world will be redeemed and made right again.

This was precisely the source of the Civil Rights movement of the 1960s: the ability of Martin Luther King, Jr., to draw upon and then to transform the personal spiritual experiences of so many Americans by his call to build a just society. Such a reconnecting of religious individualism to the public sphere has also been accomplished more recently by America's Roman Catholic bishops. Since the Second Vatican Council, their joint actions on the national scene have sought to remind us that we will survive as a people only insofar as we care for one another. They have written pastoral letters on the nuclear arms race and on the economy, and have instigated public debate on the death penalty, abortion, and United States policies in Central America. In all these efforts they have emphasized not assimilation or conformity to contemporary culture but rather a certain distance from it. And in doing so they have exemplified an independence that is characteristic of religion in our society, as well as the application of the biblical message to the concerns of the community as a whole.

II

This public role of religion, which we have been discussing from the viewpoint of individual churches, broadly corresponds to what the Founders conceived of as the exercise, on the part of citizens generally, of "public virtue." Such public virtue was of enormous importance to Americans of the Revolutionary period. To put this importance in perspective we have to recognize what the Founders understood to be the chemistry of citizenship. They all agreed that a republic which was merely a procedural democracy, where certain rules protected those who pursued their own private interests exclusively, would never succeed. The new government would survive only if its citizens could be animated by some common concern for the public good. In Federalist Paper No. 45

Madison insisted that this "public good, the real welfare of the great body of the people, is the supreme object to be pursued; and that no form of government whatever has any other value than as it may be fitted for the attainment of this object." Hence the new nation was to be built, first of all, upon a willingness of its citizens to participate directly in civic affairs, to identify their own good with the common good, and to care for and sacrifice for the public weal. "Is there no virtue among us?" asked Madison. "If there be not, no form of government can render us secure. To suppose that any form of government will secure liberty or happiness without any virtue in the people is a chimerical idea."[11]

In its pure form such republican "virtue" derived from the Renaissance political thought of Machiavelli as interpreted by Montesquieu, which insisted that humans were by nature citizens and achieved their greatest fulfillment by participation in self-government. To be completely virtuous in this sense, however, one had to be free from the petty interests of the marketplace. Hence the great enemy of true virtue was commerce, because the dependency it engendered was "corruption," by which was meant unconcern for the common good. At the time of the American Revolution such "corruption" was symbolized by the unprecedented financial and commercial ventures of England and the preoccupation of English politics with wealth, trade, and economic development. Historians of classical republicanism would even claim that it was primarily fear of this encroaching "corruption" from English parliamentary oligarchy which finally drove Americans to reject monarchy and to embrace a republic.[12] Other historians would insist that the Scottish moral philosophers Francis Hutcheson and David Hume, well known to Madison and Jefferson, made a more distinctive contribution to this concept of republican virtue. These thinkers argued that it was also a "moral sense" in all citizens that enabled them to pursue the common good. Concretely this moral sense was symbolized by the disinterested dedication of leaders like Washington, and it enabled the people in turn to select as representatives contemporary men of virtue, whose integrity and broad vision were unquestioned.[13]

But there was a second understanding of "virtue" at the time our nation was founded, one which claimed to be equally imbued with a sense of public spirit. It was best expressed perhaps by Benjamin Franklin's philosophy of successful conduct. Virtue for Franklin was a habit acquired by systematic training in choosing rationally the better course of action, not a state of consciousness so much as a means to social approval and individual economic success. The utilitarianism of this approach was ideally suited to the expanding commercial and egalitarian atmosphere of the colonies. Franklin's idea symbolized the promise of America: all persons had an equal chance to succeed on their own. Some historians have argued that the classical republicanism of Montesquieu had no appeal at all for the artisans, shopkeepers, and petty bourgeoisie who espoused Franklin's brand of virtue.[14] These middle class people had none of the independence from the market that the landed gentry had. Their interest was in property and their involvement was in commerce. They tended to be less anxious about corruption and more optimistic about profits. Pushed to extremes, this attitude simply mirrors the liberal thesis of John Locke, that would see property, not virtue, as central to American thought and politics. This is precisely the danger observed by Alexis de Tocqueville, who early in the nineteenth century saw the isolation to which this attitude could lead: "Individualism is a calm and considered feeling which disposes each citizen to isolate himself from the mass of his fellows and withdraw into the circle of family and friends; with this little society formed to his taste, he gladly leaves the greater society to look after itself."[15]

Unlike the republican strand of our culture, therefore, according to which public virtue means identifying one's own good with the common good already known, the utilitarian and individualistic strand, at least in its pure laissez-faire form, would say that the common good is what automatically emerges when each person pursues his or her own self-interest. How precisely would this happen? De Tocqueville reflected on this question and, in the context of his American experience, suggested the following:

> The doctrine of self-interest properly understood does not inspire great sacrifices, but everyday it prompts some small ones; by itself it cannot make a man virtuous, but its discipline shapes a lot of orderly, temperate, moderate, careful, and self-controlled citizens. If it does not lead the will directly to virtue, it establishes habits which unconsciously turn it that way. If the doctrine of self-interest properly understood ever came to dominate all thought about morality, no doubt extraordinary

virtues would be rarer. But I think that gross depravity would also be less common. . . . Some individuals it lowers, but mankind it raises.[16]

This comment of de Tocqueville underlines what all the Founders realized: "self-interest" and "public virtue" are not disjunctive terms: they allow for different degrees and combinations. A strong republican sense will allow a higher degree of public virtue to emerge than will a narrow self-interest. This is why the emerging political institutions of the time became so important for the new democracy. Not only did they enable the people, if they so chose, to elect officials and representatives who would place public good above local good, but they also constituted the primary means to manage conflict of interest. In Federalist Paper No. 10 Madison recognized this self-interest as one mode by which people of less public virtue might still contribute to politics. But for them to do so there would have to be some assurance that such self-interest would not corrupt. Therefore, argued Madison, checks, balances, and a separation of powers had to be built into the federal structure. Hence the need, underlined in Federalist Paper No. 51, of a "policy of supplying by opposite and rival interest, the defect of better motives."

From this brief overview it is not difficult to see that what Americans of subsequent generations inherited was a confusing compound of very different political traditions. They became as a consequence genuinely ambivalent about public life: the nation was always viewed as good, but government and politics often took on negative connotations. Robert Bellah makes the point that the language of everyday life continues in our own time to predispose toward individualism. With this language, he says, people can more easily develop loyalties to others in the context of families and small communities, but "the larger interdependencies in which people live, geographically, occupationally, and politically, are neither clearly understood nor easily encompassed by an effective sympathy. . . . When people do express a general concern for their fellow citizens as members of the national society, it is usually inspired by a hope that their more personal moral understanding can be extended to the scale of a genuinely public good."[17] In the 1950s and 1960s the Civil Rights movement provided just such a national vision, but, as I noted earlier, it was a vision that could not have been achieved without its religious inspiration. And this brings us now to a third understanding of "virtue" in American tradition, namely as devotion to the public weal originating from one's religious convictions and experience.

When de Tocqueville described the tensions he experienced between the two understandings of virtue we have been discussing, he also located elements in our culture that could neutralize these tensions and support the development of citizens predisposed to care for the common good. He called these elements the *moeurs* of Americans, from the Latin *mores*, a term he used in its most general sense "to cover the whole moral and intellectual state of a people" and "the sum of ideas that shape mental habits." But the term also had for him the more affective meaning of "habits of the heart," by which he meant practices rather than ideas and opinions, especially as applied to the strong associational life of religion and family, both of which help support political institutions and educate the citizen to a larger view than that of his purely private world.[18] For only by active involvement in common concerns can citizens overcome that sense of isolation and powerlessness that inevitably results from insecurity of life in an increasingly commercial society.[19] De Tocqueville saw religion as perhaps the most powerful of these forces in society, producing Americans whose character was especially ready to influence public life. This is why he called religion "the first of their political institutions."[20] Although it never intervened directly in government, religion elevated the basis of political freedom by safeguarding the moral standards of the people.

Religion thus functioned for de Tocqueville first of all as source of order and restraint. The "main business of religions," he insisted, "is to purify, control, and restrain that massive and exclusive taste for well-being which men acquire in times of equality." Religion shapes naked self-interest into "self-interest properly understood."[21] But religion also encourages self-sacrifice and concern for others, and, when these are expressed in public, society experiences an antidote to the selfishness of competitive individualism. Americans are consequently governed more deeply by these religious sentiments than by political institutions, because, said de Tocqueville, religion provides the primary means by which morality can enter politics. "Christianity does, it is true, teach that we must prefer others to ourselves in order to gain heaven. But Christianity also teaches that we must do good to our fellows for the love of God. That is a sublime utterance; man's mind filled with understanding of God's thought; he sees that order is God's plan, in freedom labors for this design, ever sacrificing his private interests for this wondrous ordering of all that is. . . ."[22]

It was this breadth of vision, de Tocqueville believed, which could alone prevent "virtue" from being associated solely with one's self-interest, thereby insuring that some balance would be restored between classic republicanism and utilitarian individualism, whose egoism and greed might otherwise tend to prevail. There was one condition, however: religion had to provide a framework which actually did restrain self-interest. As we shall see now, this was not the case in the Presidential election of 1984.

III

In 1982, a century and a half after de Tocqueville began his nine-month journey across America, Richard Reeves, the former political editor of *Esquire*, retraced the Frenchman's steps and compared his reflections then to the current state of our culture. On the subject of religion Reeves wrote the following: "The nation I saw no longer shared the view that public religion was necessary for the survival of republican institutions."[23] While he was personally convinced, he said, that religion should continue functioning in the public sphere, he was also convinced that the majority of Americans generally thought it should not. I think the Presidential campaign of 1984 showed how wrong Reeves was. Like most other observers, he badly underestimated the power of religion and the reasons people still have for wanting religion to influence government, however indirect that influence may be. Nor did Reeves or others even suspect what turned out to be the far more serious issue of the 1984 campaign: not *whether* religion should continue to operate through political channels, but *how* precisely it should go about doing so. Both of these, however, were the fundamental religious issues of the Presidential election, the one of principle, the other of practice and procedure. Let us look more closely at each.

Without doing here a detailed analysis of the shifts between the 1960s and 1980s, I think it fair to say that the issue of prin-

ciple surfaced with such clarity during the 1984 campaign because for years both secularist ideology as well as a certain
radically individualistic religion had conspired to treat religion
as a purely private affair. It was natural, of course, that convinced secularists should think religious values suspect and
want them excluded from determination of public policy. The
perseverance of these values in secular society constituted an
embarrassment, alleviated only partially by insisting that any
moral judgments based on them simply reflected private interests and opinions. In no sense, however, ought these religious values to become the basis for public moral consensus.
Hence it was important for the secularist to have an interpretation of church-state separation so strict that it would altogether
exclude religious groups from influencing government, even
through the most ordinary political channels.[24] In addition to
the secularist, however, there was also the religious individualist, who in principle held aloof from the public church. This
type could either be the old style conservative fundamentalist
or the new style religious mystic. The latter, coming out of the
1960s, pursued inner freedom and a self-reflecting experience
of God, and was deeply suspicious of social commitments and
institutional religion in any form. The former, inheritor of the
old revivalist tradition, wanted total certitude in matters of
faith, conceived of God as external to the world, and was
deeply suspicious of any talk of divine involvement in worldly
affairs. Secularists found the privatizing tendencies of these
two opposite poles highly compatible with their concept of
American society: neither secularist nor individualist wanted
any religious presence in the public sphere.[25] In the election
of 1960, John F. Kennedy took great pains to assure both secularist and religious individualist that his Roman Catholicism
was an inner faith and should in no sense be identified with
his candidacy. He insisted that he would have not even the
remotest external ties with his church's authorities, and would
vigorously resist any church influence on either his political
policies or his constitutional duties.[26] Kennedy seems to have
believed in a separation of church and state so absolute as to
rule out any role at all for religion in discussions of public policy. In his mind churches could have no agenda in the political
realm beyond lobbying for their own sectarian interests.

Sixteen years later, however, in the election of 1976, it became
clear that, unlike Kennedy, Jimmy Carter saw no problem with

the historic dialogue between religion and politics, even though, like Kennedy, he favored a strong separation of church and state. Moreover, because he faced a peculiar crisis of trust and confidence inherited from Lyndon Johnson and Richard Nixon, Carter felt compelled to use his personal religion to authenticate his own character. While emphasizing that as President he would be prohibited by the Constitution from basing public policy on religious preferences, he did not hesitate to point to his commitment as a born-again Christian, as well as to the larger role that faith in Christ played in his public life, freely acknowledging that he prayed daily, particularly when making important decisions. During the four years of his Presidency religion remained a continuing background factor in his policy-making and underlined his initiatives in human rights, peace, and energy.[27]

Jimmy Carter's election was a watershed, marking the emergence, as an important political factor, of that branch of individualist religion represented by evangelical Protestantism. On many political issues this branch was both liberal and progressive, though in religious matters usually very conservative. Beginning in the early 1970s its members had gradually begun to reconnect themselves to the public church, so that by 1976 the October 25th issue of *Newsweek* could designate that year as " the year of the evangelicals." However, not all evangelicals could support a Democrat like Carter. An ultra-conservative political offshoot of the branch began to emerge in the mid-1970s, and toward the end of the decade could be clearly identified under the name of the "Moral Majority" and the leadership of Jerry Falwell. Their objective was to take into the public sphere all their private faith grievances that had been building up over the years. While there is general agreement that on the national level they could take little credit for the 1980 Republican landslide, they nevertheless rode the anti-abortion wave that year and rallied right-wing fundamentalist support for Ronald Reagan.[28] Their real strength in 1980 appeared on the state level, where they were able to target for defeat certain liberal Democratic U.S. Senators and to put in their place candidates who supported their positions on issues ranging from abortion to strong national defense.

All was very different in 1984. For the Moral Majority now had national status and were defending a principle as well as advocating specific legislative and administrative action. That principle, articulated again and again by Ronald Reagan, is that in the United States politics and religion are interrelated. Whether or not the President was more concerned here with a political agenda than with a religious conviction, he was nevertheless pointing to a simple historical fact: the values of the vast majority of American citizens are deeply rooted in religion and so must in some way inevitably inform politics. Positively, this principle states that all religious convictions are politically relevant. But in American society it has a negative corollary: no religious conviction can declare itself politically normative. Reagan and the Moral Majority eagerly embraced the positive side of this principle. In so doing they enabled fundamentalists to take seriously for the first time what mainline churches had always believed, namely that there is an interdependence not only between personal faith and the believing community, but also between both of these and the public spheres of national and local politics.

In practice, however, the Moral Majority's emphasis upon the positive side of this principle proved highly disruptive, because they refused to recognize the negative corollary. What they wanted, they said, was to appeal to religiously based public values and so alert people to the crisis of moral decadence facing the nation, especially the weakening of the family. How they actually did this, however, (about which more in a moment) so alienated other Americans, secular as well as religious, that the importance of the principle they defended was partially lost. This was because fundamentalists were not searching for some new national consensus, built upon values widely shared by believing communities. Their mistake was to believe that such public consensus was already in place, and that this justified the strongarm tactics they chose to use against the "moral minority." For in their eyes there could be no religious tolerance of any such minority value system.

To understand this outlook one has to recognize that in the present century American culture had changed rapidly and many American values changed with it, and that this upset them deeply. Politics for them was thus simply a weapon, to be used to impose upon the country as a whole an older, more simplified version of national morality. Generally this included, but was not limited to, the criminalization of abortion, the legalization of prayer in public schools, opposition to feminism and the equal rights amendment, and an emphasis upon the evils of homosexuality and the use of busing to insure racial integration. To be against a return to such "tradition" was in their minds to be against "religion." Hence when Ronald Reagan warned in the election year that America was "losing her religious and moral bearings," and called for a "rebirth of freedom and faith," this was the national morality he was advocating. He was not talking about the nuclear arms buildup or racial inequality as moral problems, nor did he focus on hunger and poverty and social justice at home, nor on human rights issues in South Africa and Latin America. For none of these were religious values as religion had now come to be defined by right-wing Protestant fundamentalism.

What was disruptive, therefore, in the interaction of religion and politics during the 1984 election year was not the *fact* of interaction but the *mode* of interaction; not the entry of the Moral Majority into the public forum but the intolerance which they brought with them. It was their religious values and theirs alone which were to be normative for the nation. Even though in their most general formulations some of these, such as the values of family life, are common to all religious institutions, it was not these general formulations that were to be normative but a very specific sectarian version of them.

Words like "tolerance"and "civility" do, of course, carry negative connotations, sometimes denoting a measure of distance from one's own faith rather than deep commitment to it, mixed with some doubt and uncertainty perhaps, making accommodation to another's religion relatively easy.[29] But tolerance and civility need not at all convey the sense that "one religion is as good as another." As Martin Marty has observed, following Gabriel Marcel, such words ought rather refer to the respect that is due in a pluralistic society to the strong convictions of others precisely because one's own convictions are equally strong. When such different sets of convictions are articulated in the public arena, they naturally constitute conflicting interest groups. But if these groups use political weapons to coerce others by force of numbers, then they immediately constitute what the Founders called "factions," people devoid of public virtue, who refuse to participate in common discussions for a common good, but seek only to advance their narrow private concerns and those of their group. Does this mean that in times of rapid cultural change, there will be a loss of some shared values and moral certitudes? Of course. But then it is the task of public virtue not only to guard debate on these values and prevent imposition of simplified solutions on complex problems, but also to heal incivility and enable those who disagree to continue to live and work and cooperate together.[30]

It was one of the misfortunes of the Democrats in the 1984 election to have been so alarmed by the fundamentalist content given by Republicans to the term "religion" that they failed to comprehend the importance for the electorate of the principle of the public church. They failed to take seriously the connections the American public makes between religious convictions, moral values, and public policy. This is ironic, because both Walter Mondale and Geraldine Ferraro are religious people devoted to religious values, especially the importance of family life — as are the majority of those who have historically constituted the Democratic coalition. But neither would grant explicitly enough the principle of the public church, even though they themselves were defending values which clearly originated in their Christian faith, such as concern for the poor and minorities, and justice for all groups in society. Ultimately religious values lay behind their political positions against the unfairness of budget cuts that increased dependency of the poor on the rich, against government leniency toward those who pollute the environment, and against increased spending by the military at the expense of social services. But rarely, in terms of their overall political positions, did they relate any of these values to what was obviously their source. On the contrary, when challenged on specific issues, such as abortion, both almost always insisted that religion was a private affair between the individual and God.[31] Meanwhile "religion" was coming more and more to mean what the New Right said it meant. Complex cultural causes of the family's increased social instability were traced to traditional Democratic support of individual freedoms, especially the removal of censorship, civil rights for homosexuals, sex education of children, opposition to prayer in public schools, and the decriminalization of abortion. All of these now became examples of irreligion.

Nowhere did this problem appear more clearly in the campaign than in discussions of the very painful question of abortion. Both Reagan and Mondale declared themselves personally opposed to abortion because of their religious beliefs. But Reagan advocated immediate action on these beliefs by supporting a constitutional amendment to criminalize abortion, thereby vindicating once again the nexus between religion and politics. In practice, of course, such criminalization would do away with public debate altogether, focusing only on the rights of the fetus and ignoring the enormous complexity of the problem—including the meaning of privacy and individual freedom, as well as the compelling moral imperative experienced by many to alleviate situations that are oppressive and harmful to women. Mondale took a much more nuanced position, holding that where no national consensus exists on the evil of abortion, the law should be used to mediate the conflict, not to remove it prematurely from the public forum. While this is a reasoned position, Mondale seems never to have felt that his religious convictions had any contribution to make to the public debate he encouraged. Many of his supporters wondered why he was not more consistent in his overall position. Did he not feel compelled, they asked, to argue for some positive action to promote what he believed as a Christian to be the good of the nation?

This was the question often put to Geraldine Ferraro and Mario Cuomo, both Roman Catholics, both opposed like Mondale to a constitutional amendment, yet both loyal to their church's official position that abortion is always an intrinsic moral evil.[32] Only Cuomo developed a reasoned answer. An anti-abortion amendment, he said, would be unworkable as public policy, because without a national consensus such negative legislation would only generate widespread contempt for the law and duplicate the lawlessness of Prohibition. The common good would suffer if politicians did not exercise some self-restraint in translating their moral convictions into coercive law. What he proposed instead, as a political strategy, were public programs that would support the freedom of women who would otherwise have abortions to have their children and then either keep them or place them in adoption. He agreed that the witness of Catholic bishops ought to be outspoken and courageous, arguing in public the evils of abortion for both individual and community and proposing public remedies. But he insisted that a Catholic politician need not be in total agreement with the bishops when it comes to prudent decisions on how precisely to avoid these evils and promote the common good. For, unlike bishops, politicians take an oath to preserve the Constitution, which has guaranteed freedom to do many things forbidden by Catholic teaching, including the right to divorce and remarry, the right to use contraceptives, and now the right to have an abortion. More importantly, continued Cuomo, Catholic politicians ought to see a solution to the abortion question as part of a larger and more pressing political agenda: "The work of creating a society where the right to life doesn't end at the moment of birth; where an infant isn't helped into a world that doesn't care if it's fed properly, housed decently, educated adequately; where the blind or retarded child isn't condemned to exist rather than empowered to live."[33]

IV

I have argued in this chapter that religion is alive and well in the United States today and that, insofar as it is expressed in a public church, its role is to exercise public virtue. Positively, this means that individuals and communities that constitute such a church will seek to add the concerns of biblical religion to controversial questions of the common good. Negatively, it means that such an exercise of public witness must not degenerate into just another political lobby. For to act as a public church means to engage in public discourse, advancing reasoned argument based on the common good to justify positions on national morality. Religious groups whose only public role is to form voting blocks to support candidates who promise to support the group's narrow interests ignore both their authentic role to proclaim a message of values and the role of the state to work for the common good of all. In matters of religion long-term conversion of heart is always to be preferred to stonewalling. No single religious community can therefore take it for granted that the blueprint they espouse for national morality constitutes a complete answer to complex societal problems. Nor can they ever presume that their message, however inspiring and noble, is exempt either from public scrutiny and argument or from the slow procedures of the democratic process.[34]

Right-wing fundamentalists made such a presumption in the 1984 Presidential campaign. Their sudden influence took completely by surprise those who opposed a role for religion in politics or who thought the connection between them finally dormant or dead.[35] But what alarmed religious-minded people most was not their entry into the public sphere but their intolerance and incivility, since they saw these as threats to the basic relationship in principle between these two powerful forces of society. For members of the public church that relationship has always had two presuppositions. First, social integration in a pluralist society requires more than a democratic process that muddles through by evading conflicts of conscience, personal dignity, and ultimate meanings. These must be grappled with publicly if citizens are to define at any given time the elements of a just social order. By participating in such struggle to locate the common good, the public church seeks to be the primary means by which morality and moral discourse enter politics. The second presupposition is corollary to the first: in the course of such efforts religious groups may have to accept the propagation of what they may individually regard as morally wrong. This does not mean that they have to be any less committed to their ideals, but simply that they live in a free and pluralistic society, and so must respect the good faith of those who hold moral positions different from their own.

This second presupposition explains why communities in the public church must be so attentive that their own properly biblical concerns are translated into reasoned argument, appropriate to civic discourse and accessible to all, believer and unbeliever alike. For the moral positions held by the majority of citizens at any given time may not in fact be reasoned at all. The public church is thus in a position to offer perhaps the strongest counterbalance to what social analysts now fear most in Western liberal societies, namely that moral judgments will be advanced without any basis in fundamental beliefs about the human person or the nature of human society. Indeed, the great danger in American society today is that policies will be formed from an amalgam of personal preferences and feelings.

This danger is best illustrated by the claims of supporters of the so-called "therapeutic" personality, which has become the dominant form taken in post-war America by the utilitarian and individualistic ethos of the past. While proponents of the therapeutic point of view are not opposed to morality, they locate its center in the autonomous individual, not in the common good of society. As much as they can, therapeutics resist any moral demands made on them by others, and are generally suspicious or cynical about moral conviction as the inner dynamic of the social order. They are intent upon "finding themselves," seeking pleasure, personal self-control and psychic balance, are without enthusiasm for causes of any kind, and, as self-sufficient individuals, they want political institutions off their backs.[36] Yet even these highly privatized personalities can be open to the voice of the public church. The reason is that they still think in terms of commitments—from marriage and work to political and religious involvement—insofar as these are presented as enhancements of their sense of individual well-being rather than as moral imperatives.

Such commitments are precisely what the public church must build upon if this new type of American individualist is to be reconnected to the political process. In contrast to the private church, which like the family provides a comfortable haven from worldly cares, the public church must appeal in its political argument to that search for larger meanings that goes on even at the heart of the therapeutic personality. For only breadth of vision can finally transform private virtue, associated exclusively with self-interest, into public virtue directed toward the common good. In this sense the public church remains today the primary means whereby private morality can be refocused upon the public sphere, and whereby a balance can be struck between the exercise of public responsibility in its fullest sense and that search for personal well-being that of itself tends totally to privatize.

2

The Churches in
A Benevolent State

When they first became law in 1791, the Establishment and Free Exercise Clauses of the First Amendment constituted a relationship between the churches and government which was unique in the world of that time, an achievement of political intelligence which was to have momentous consequences. One historian has said that "on the administration side, the two most profound revolutions which have occurred in the entire history of the church have been these: first, the change of the church, in the fourth century, from a voluntary society . . . to a society conceived as necessarily co-extensive with the civil community and endowed with the power to enforce the adherence of all members of the civil community; second, the reversal of this change . . . in America."[1]

This reversal had been carefully scrutinized and discussed in America long before it was codified into law. Initially it was thought of as an experiment with a very important structure of civil society: institutional religion. As such it involved risk, for a religion mediates the values and ideals of a society just as effectively as do institutions which are political, economic, or educational. This risk continues today and involves a three-fold commitment: to religious pluralism, to religious freedom, and to government neutrality. In this chapter I shall seek to analyze each of these commitments in turn.

Before we begin, however, let me make one important observation. To designate our general discussion area as that of church and state can be misleading. The problem as it exists in America is not so much a relationship between two institutions as one between two outlooks of the individual, his outlook as citizen and his outlook as member of a religious denomination. For in a democracy, where sovereignty resides in the people, the struggle between God and Caesar must necessarily be internalized. To project it outward, to deal with it as wholly objective, is to miss its key dimension. What we are really dealing with in America is a competition between two religions, the one civil, the other denominational. It is up to the individual citizen to balance these two sets of claims, to decide upon the extent of his allegiance to each.[2] Historically our nation has attempted through its ideals and goals to bind the people together under God, giving them, however unsuccessfully at times, a genuine apprehension of God's transcendent reality. Americans have thus tended to find the symbols of ultimate meaning not only in their churches but also in their country. Hence the so-called "conflict between church and state" is basically an attempt by citizens with allegiance to both institutions to evaluate and criticize the one by criteria received from the other. We should not be surprised, then, to find tensions in this area which are perennial, built as they are into the whole fabric of our society. With this important observation as preamble, let us turn now to the first of the three commitments I just mentioned, namely, our commitment to religious pluralism.

I

Religious pluralism was a fact in America long before it became an object of belief. This was not because the various religious bodies which took root in the Colonies were particularly tolerant of each other. On the contrary, they seem all to have behaved in what came later to be called "typical sectarian fashion," each one claiming exclusively to be "the Church," and absolutizing those particularities in doctrine and practice which distinguished it from other Christian groups. The reason there was at the same time so much religious freedom in the Colonies was chiefly due to the openness and sparsely settled nature of the country: the nonconformist simply moved away into that vast space where deviance immediately became orthodoxy. Groups holding divergent and incompatible views on religious questions thus gradually came to coexist in different parts of the country. As a sense of national community grew, giving birth to political consensus in resistance to Great Britain, disagreement on things religious came to be regarded as less and less important. The two principal movements in American Christianity at the time, moreover, rationalism and pietism, tended to encourage this growing belief that formal differences in doctrine and worship were not of ultimate importance. Rationalists like Franklin and Jefferson believed that the essentials of any religion could be reduced to a common set of intellectual propositions regarding God, immortality, and the life of virtue. Pietists, on the other hand, in the tradition of John Wesley, were convinced that spiritual nourishment had to be found in experience, not in the barren intellectualism of creeds, doctrine, and theology. Thus rationalists appealed to the head and pietists to the heart to reach the same conclusion at the very time that, for geographic reasons, many different sects were enjoying relatively peaceful coexistence.[3]

This *de facto* pluralism meant that none of the dominant churches was in a position to press for religious uniformity. Indeed, there was a practical necessity for all of them to connive at religious variety; because no single church could make a successful bid for national establishment, it was to the self-interest of each to be tolerant of all in order to guarantee such toleration for itself. The motivation was thus purely pragmatic; very few church pronouncements at the time articulated any positive ideological thrust for toleration. Churches did not really "contribute to religious liberty, they stumbled into it, they were compelled into it, they accepted it at last because they had to, or because they saw its strategic value."[4] This *de facto* pluralism likewise made one other conclusion unavoidable: since so many sects, holding very different beliefs, were able to coexist in peace, it followed that uniformity of religious practice was obviously not essential to the public welfare, something hitherto assumed to be true for centuries by all the countries of Western Europe. It was this last realization, that religious solidarity was not needed to stabilize the social order, which paved the way for the Establishment and Free Exercise Clauses of the First Amendment.

"Congress shall make no law respecting an establishment of religion, or prohibiting the free exercise thereof." These clauses did not create a new idea, but were rather the legal recognition of an actual state of things which had come to be seen as practically unavoidable. The Founders wanted to formulate a principle which would guarantee the participation of all churches in the common social unity of the republic, while at the same time not compromising those distinctive modes of worship and belief proper to each. The First Amendment was therefore conceived to be an experiment in the political realm, an effort to strengthen the new nation by excluding from government concern all religious differences among its people. At the time it was by no means certain that the experiment would be successful, that is to say, that it would necessarily be conducive to public peace and order. Writing in 1785, six years before the Amendment's adoption, Jefferson reminded his State of Virginia that the States of Pennsylvania and New York had long had an official policy of no-establishment. "The experiment was new and doubtful when they made it," he said. "It has answered beyond conception. They flourish infinitely. Religion is well supported; of various kinds, indeed, but all good enough; all sufficient to preserve peace and order. . . ."[5] Speaking on this same question in 1808, seventeen years after the Amendment's adoption, Jefferson could say: "We have solved by fair experiment, the great and interesting question whether freedom of religion is compatible with order in government, and obedience to the laws." [6] Somewhere, then, within the twenty-three year period between these two statements, an ideological revolution took place which finally made the experiment of religious pluralism acceptable in theory as well as in practice. What was responsible for this ideological shift?

According to Sidney Mead, it was generally recognized at the time that establishment in other countries rested on two basic assumptions: first, that the well-being of society depended upon a body of shared religious beliefs—the nature of the human person, his place in the cosmos, his destiny, and his conduct toward his fellows—and second, that the only way to guarantee the inculcation of these necessary beliefs was to put the coercive power of the state behind the institution responsible for their inculcation. Now what gradually became clear to statesmen and clergy alike was that acceptance of religious pluralism meant giving up not the first assumption but only the second, namely that the state must use its coercive power to inculcate religious belief. The essence of the ideological shift was therefore the rejection of coercion in favor of persuasion.

With the exception of a few extreme deists and agnostics, the Founders never interpreted the principle of uncoerced consent to mean that government ought to be indifferent to religion, since from religion came truths essential for public order and stability. The principle meant rather that responsibility for inculcating these truths, thought to be common to every religion, rested with the churches alone, to be carried out in whatever ways individual churches wished, relying upon persuasion, however, and not upon the government's coercive power. We should note too that this ideological shift was in many ways the natural extension into the religious sphere of the eighteenth century's key idea that free consent was the only rational basis for organizing civil government. The two movements we mentioned earlier, for example, rationalism and pietism, both wanted to promote this extension, though for very different reasons, the one basing autonomy in religious matters upon the primacy of reason in weighing evidence, the other upon the direct guidance of the Holy Spirit and the reading of Sacred Scripture.[7]

All the Protestant churches gradually came to accept this ideology for pluralism, reformulating it to fit their respective traditions which originally (with the exception of the Baptists) contained little or no theoretical justification for it. Pluralism was eventually justified as a new outward manifestation of traditional Protestant anti-authoritarianism, fostering anew traditional Protestant virtues of voluntarism and privatism. One far-reaching result of such reformulation was a new organizational form for Protestant churches. They began to think of themselves eventually as "denominations," groups which neither claimed to be exclusively "the Church" nor absolutized the peculiarities which distinguished them from other groups. Unlike a "sect," a "denomination" recognized itself as finite witness to the Christian gospel, imperfect in knowledge and authority as well as in practice. Henceforth, it was thought, the state could never become involved in any way in the religious sphere without immediately threatening the free church system either by patronizing some churches or by coercing all.[8]

Jews and Roman Catholics were not unaffected by this nineteenth-century rationalization of religious pluralism. American Jews tended to view their society and culture both then and later as "ambiguous mixtures of secularism and Christianity."[9] They have generally preferred strong religious pluralism and strict government neutrality, not from some ideology of church-state relations but from their experience of Jewish history. They know that whenever a government has been supportive of one or another Christian church in the past, Jews have invariably had to put up with some discomfort, and not infrequently with much worse. For such supportive relationships usually involve at least some intolerance toward religious minorities, precisely because the importance of religious differences is thereby increased. Jews have learned from bitter experience that it is wise to minimize these differences.[10] Hence in America, with the possible exception of Orthodox Jews, they have traditionally given strong support to Protestant voluntarism and privatism, even though Judaism itself is the most normative of religions.

Like Jews, Roman Catholics were a very small minority when religious pluralism was being given its ideological underpinning. Unlike Jews, however, Catholics could not accept the militant privatism of the Protestant denominations, because their tradition has consistenly favored cooperative arrangements between governments and religious groups. For a Catholic, government ought to have an interest in the relationship of its citizens to God. Mutually advantageous arrangements should therefore be worked out pragmatically. This ought to be especially true in the United States, where the sovereignty of God in human life had always been publicly recognized. Hence the Catholic position is that the pluralism guaranteed by the First Amendment cannot be understood to assert or imply that the nature of a religious organization is such that it inherently demands the most absolute separation of church and state. Cooperation may never become actual, but it must indeed be possible, albeit on a nondiscriminatory basis. John Courtney Murray used to say that in one sense it is irrelevant what the Founders originally thought about such cooperation. "What is in question is the meaning and the content of the first of our American prejudices, not its genesis." The Catholic "rejects the notion that any of these sectarian theses enter into the content or implications of the First Amendment in such wise as to demand the assent of all American Citizens. If this were the case, the very article that bars any establishment of religion would somehow establish one."[11]

These reactions of Christians and Jews to the First Amendment show that, although all have welcomed in practice the guarantees of free exercise and no-establishment, each tradition has had its problems vis-à-vis the others in integrating the Amendment into its own history. In fact, one aspect of the original ideological shift has never been adequately integrated.

Sidney Mead calls it the Trojan horse in the citadel of religious pluralism. The dilemma stems from the fact that the legal and political forms of this pluralism were worked out not by the clergy, but by the statesmen who by and large were disciples of the Enlightenment. As we saw earlier, these statesmen believed that churches (or "sects" as they usually called them) should flourish in America because it was important for the general welfare. That is to say, they believed that all churches held and taught in common the "essentials of every religion," and that these essentials were not only relevant but vital for the health of the nation. This implied, of course, that what was not commonly held was neither relevant nor vital. Whatever a religious group might hold as a peculiar tenet of its own faith, which made it distinct from other groups and constituted the reason for its separate existence, was thought to be at best only of indirect value to the republic. Hence "all the spectacular success of the free churches in America in effecting numerical growth and geographic expansion . . . has taken place under this Damoclean sword — the haunting suspicion that somehow relevance to the general welfare decreased in proportion to sectarian success."[12]

This Damoclean sword has had some very far-reaching consequences for the churches in this pluralistic land. Spiritual compartmentalization is one consequence, noted even in the last century by Alexis de Tocqueville. Speaking specifically of Roman Catholics, he said that they "have divided the world of the mind into two parts; in one are revealed dogmas to which they submit without discussion; political truth finds its place in the other half, which they think God has left to man's free investigation. Thus American Catholics are both the most obedient of the faithful and the most independent citizens."[13] A second consequence is the phenomenon known as civil religion: insofar as individual denominations have relinquished their claims to be "the Church," the nation itself has tended more and more to assume this function, speaking with far greater authority than purely voluntary ecclesiastical societies.

The third consequence, however, is the most serious: the churches have become confused in regard to what should be their primary religious witness in a pluralistic land. For institutional religion usually suffers from one of two types of irrelevance: either it retains meaning for its members on the personal level but loses it for society at large, or it manages to be historically relevant in the public realm but of little or no significance for the needs of ordinary people. This is because the American value system has always been a mixture of the secular and the sacred, and American religion has generally exhibited the same sort of value mix. Churches and synagogues were able to cope so easily with the secularization of the twentieth century precisely because to a certain extent they had incorporated many of society's secular values into their own systems of thought and bureaucratic structures, thereby exposing themselves to the dilemma of religious witness I just mentioned. Religion was usually given a very specific role as a Sunday affair. To mention it on weekdays meant that one was expected to speak in terms of a morality acceptable to the nation as a whole, or not to speak at all.

II

When we consider now our second commitment, to religious freedom, it is clear that this has to be seen as an extension of our commitment to religious pluralism. At the start of our history the Establishment and Free Exercise Clauses were understood to prescribe a mutual independence: religion was to be safeguarded from the power of the state, and political society was to be safeguarded from interference by organized religion. For the first time in the memory of the West a nation's churches were to be insulated from the intervention of its government, whether this intervention be used to establish religion or to restrain its practice. The gain for the churches was, of course, an increase in their freedom. But there was gain for the state as well, namely the avoidance of political strife along religious lines, since common experience made it clear that whenever religion becomes a political issue, it invariably exhibits qualities that are both explosive and divisive.[14] Government thus set limits to those absolutist tendencies endemic to every church, preventing any single one from becoming a monopoly and imposing its particular form on the people. Here in America the state could neither restrict nor become captive to any religious vision, yet each religious vision could flourish and expand insofar as it relied upon persuasion and not upon force. In claiming freedom for themselves, religious groups would have to affirm equal freedom for others, whatever their beliefs might be.

I said at the start that these religion clauses were an extraordinary achievement of political intelligence, and so they were. The leitmotiv running through the process of their adoption was the American impulse toward freedom, both political and religious. This impulse brought an emphatic reaffirmation of the distinction between the religious and political orders, a distinction quite common in medieval Christendom, but almost completely lost to Europe through the rise of national monarchies and the development of royal absolutism. One reason Americans embraced the distinction so strongly was that they inherited it through English common law, where it had somehow managed to survive. But the chief reason was its power to allay the fears of statesmen like Madison and Jefferson that too much church would corrupt the state, and the fears of ministers like Roger Williams that too much state could corrupt the church. Such fears made both groups eager to establish freedom in this area as the rule. They therefore pressed the distinction between spiritual and temporal—to an exaggerated degree perhaps, but, as John Courtney Murray once said, government rarely appears to better advantage than when passing self-denying ordinances. In any event, everyone then and since has agreed that exaggerating the distinction is a danger much to be preferred to its abolition.[15]

The view I have just sketched of religious freedom makes for a very idyllic picture indeed. The single function of government is to see to it that the guarantee of this freedom is effective. Yet the most complex historical and legal difficulties have arisen whenever government has sought to exercise this function. The reason is that the Founders never spelled out precisely *how* such religious freedom was to be guaranteed, nor how the promotion of such freedom was to be distinguished from the promotion of religious belief. Some say they were deliberately ambiguous, either because they themselves could not agree, or because they saw a positive advantage in leaving the question open for future generations. If so, then they succeeded. The question is indeed open, many arguing that the best way to guarantee religious freedom is to make the distinction between church and state as complete as humanly possible, and to understand the Establishment Clause as "build-

ing up a wall of separation" between the two. This wall metaphor was used almost casually by Thomas Jefferson in an 1802
letter to the Baptist Association of Danbury, Connecticut,[16] yet
it has had, as we shall see, some fateful consequences for the
interpretation of the First Amendment.

A very different metaphor was chosen by James Madison,
who spoke thirty years later about "the line of separation between the rights of religion and Civil authority."[17] The image
of a "line" has the advantage of being much more flexible than
that of a "wall," its elements constantly changing so as to make
it difficult, as Madison noted, to trace with such distinctness
as to avoid collisions and doubts. Hence the line image does
not conjure up a confrontation between two antagonistic institutions, separated for all time by an impregnable barrier which
must be defended by one and attacked by the other. Madison's
metaphor makes it much easier to see that what is really the
case is that Americans, who in fact belong as individuals to
both institutions, are engaged in a common quest to determine
where the line is to be drawn at any particular point in the
nation's history. Supreme Court decisions also assume a different image when looked at through Madison's eyes: they are
not like large stones mortared into a solid wall, but like points
where the line appears to the majority of Justices to be fixed
at any given time.[18]

It is indeed quite surprising that two figures of speech, nowhere in the Constitution, could so color its interpretation. The
wall image first appeared in the 1878 *Reynolds* case, though it
did not play any direct role there. Chief Justice Waite wanted
to use another phrase in Jefferson's letter to support his decision and could not edit out "the wall."[19] It did not reappear
until 1948, when Justice Black, quoting *Reynolds*, used it to explain the Establishment Clause in *Everson*: "The First Amendment has erected a wall between church and state. That wall
must be kept high and impregnable. We could not approve
the slightest breach."[20] Black is generally believed to have been
motivated here by his constitutional absolutism. But Charles
Reich has argued that one must distinguish Black's fear of flexible standards that are easily bent from his desire that the Constitution keep pace with a changing society. Black recognized,
Reich argues, that there was no such thing as a static meaning
for constitutional provisions. The "absolutes" he insisted on
are dynamic ones, open to the changing conditions and under-

standings of the day. He believed that "in constitutions, constancy requires change."[21]

In any event, whether Black intended rigidity or not, the metaphor provoked a mixed reaction in subsequent decisions. Justice Reed complained a year after *Everson*: "A rule of law should not be drawn from a figure of speech."[22] Justice Stewart echoed him in l962: "I think the Court's task . . . is not responsibly aided by the uncritical invocation of metaphors like the 'wall of separation,' a phrase nowhere to be found in the Constitution."[23] Ten years earlier Justice Jackson had had the opposite complaint: "The wall which the Court was professing to erect between Church and State has become even more warped and twisted than I expected."[24] It was not until 1977 that this complaint was voiced again. Justice Stevens wrote that year: "What should be a 'high and impregnable' wall between church and state, has been reduced to a 'blurred, indistinct and variable barrier.'"[25]

In contrast, the movable line metaphor, pointing to flexibility, appears to be used more casually. Justice Douglas set the tone in 1952: "The First Amendment, however, does not say that in every and all respects there shall be a separation of Church and State. Rather, it studiously defines the manner, the specific ways, in which there shall be no concert or union or dependency one on the other. That is the common sense of the matter. Otherwise the state and religion would be aliens to each other—hostile, suspicious, and even unfriendly."[26] In the 1963 *Schempp* case Justice Brennan stated: "The fact is that the line which separates the secular from the sectarian in American life is elusive." Yet there is a "line we must draw between the permissible and the impermissible."[27] Six years later Justice White had to admit: "*Everson* and later cases have shown that the line between state neutrality to religion and state support of religion is not easy to locate."[28] Chief Justice Burger has used the metaphor twice, in 1970 and 1971:

> The course of constitutional neutrality in this area cannot be an absolutely straight line; rigidity could well defeat the basic purpose of these provisions, which is to insure that no religion be sponsored or favored, none commanded, and none inhibited. The general principle deductible from the First Amendment and all that has been said by the Court is this: that we will not tolerate either governmentally established religion or governmental interference with religion. Short of these expressly pro-

scribed governmental acts there is room for play in the joints productive of a benevolent neutrality which will permit religious exercise to exist without sponsorship and without interference. . . . No perfect absolute separation is really possible.[29]

Candor compels acknowledgement [that] we can only dimly perceive the lines of demarcation in this extraordinarily sensitive area of constitutional law. . . . In the absence of precisely stated constitutional prohibitions, we must draw lines . . . .[30]

I shall discuss Burger's "benevolent neutrality" concept presently. Just now I am concerned with the impact of the "wall" and "line" images upon the nation's commitment to religious freedom. There are two root questions to be dealt with: first, what is the constitutional duty regarding freedom of religion, and second, what is religion? The Court began to answer to the first question in 1940 when Justice Roberts wrote in *Cantwell* v. *Connecticut* that "the Amendment embraces two concepts, — freedom to believe and freedom to act. The first is absolute but, in the nature of things, the second cannot be." But it was not until 1961 that the Court was asked a more concrete question: whether a Pennsylvania Sunday closing law could impose economic loss on sabbatarians whose religious belief required them to close also on Saturday. Yes, replied the Court, because this burden is indirect (no one was forced to work on Saturday), and without it Pennsylvania could not accomplish its purpose of having everyone rest on the same day.[31]

Justice Brennan strongly disagreed with this holding, and two years later wrote an opinion in *Sherbert* v. *Verner* which has become the controlling constitutional law. Even a burden which is indirect can in fact be extremely heavy, said Brennan, and when it is, then a compelling state interest is needed to justify it. Mrs. Sherbert, a Seventh-Day Adventist in South Carolina, had been discharged by her employer for refusal to work on Saturday, and was subsequently disqualified from the state's unemployment compensation under a statute requiring her to accept suitable work when offered. South Carolina's interest in preventing fraudulent claims, insisted Brennan, was not enough to justify such a substantial infringement of Mrs. Sherbert's right of free-exercise. For this right was fundamental, like the right to free-speech, and its limitation must pass the tests of necessity and the unavailability of alternative means.[32]

Does *Sherbert* mean, then, that religious motives are to be accorded better treatment than non-religious? This was clearly the thrust of Chief Justice Burger's 1972 opinion in *Wisconsin v. Yoder*. The Amish sect in Wisconsin refused to allow their children to attend school beyond the eighth grade, thereby disobeying a state law requiring school attendance until age 16. The state did not show, the Court said, how its heavy interest in compulsory education would be advanced by compelling two more years of education for the children in violation of Amish religious belief. The issue was therefore whether the Amish religious faith and mode of life were indeed inseparable. For "if the Amish asserted their claims because of their subjective evaluation and rejection of the contemporary secular values accepted by the majority. . . . their claims would not rest on a religious basis."[33] While the Court could give no weight at all to such secular considerations, the Amish mode of life was accorded high deference because it was found to be a deep religious conviction.

The constitutional duty of government toward religion is consequently one of care for religious freedom. "That the central value embodied in the First Amendment . . . is the safeguarding of an individual's right to free exercise of his religion has been consistently recognized."[34] This conclusion naturally leads us to the second question with which the Court has had to grapple: how is "religion" to be defined? The theistic orientation of classical Western thought characterized the first effort at definition, which was made in an 1890 polygamy case: "The term 'religion' has reference to one's views on his relation to his Creator and to the obligations they impose of reverence for his being, and of obedience to his will."[35] Chief Justice Hughes's definition in 1931 was substantially the same: "The essence of religion is belief in a relation to God involving duties superior to those arising from any human relation."[36] Steps toward better definition were taken gradually. In 1944 Justice Douglas ruled in *United States* v. *Ballard*: "Men may believe what they cannot prove. They may not be put to proof of their religious doctrines or beliefs. . . . Yet the fact that they may be beyond the ken of mortals does not mean that they can be made suspect before the law."[37] Since there could be no inquiry into the truth or falsity of religious claims, the only question was whether the belief was sincerely held. Protection of religious freedom thus extended to the most unorthodox of

beliefs, and the parameters of "religion" were not to be confined to the narrow boundaries of traditional practices.

Ballard foreshadowed Justice Black's famous footnote in a
1961 case, which declared that "among religions in this country which do not teach what would generally be considered
a belief in the existence of God are Buddhism, Taoism, Ethical
Culture, Secular Humanism and others."[38] The context of this
remark was a Maryland requirement that one Roy Torcaso
could not receive his commission as a notary public unless he
took an oath affirming his belief in God. Black agreed that the
Maryland statute favored those who would say they believed
in the existence of God, and that this violated Torcaso's
freedom of religion. Four years later a youth named Daniel An-
drew Seeger claimed that same violation by §6 (j) of the 1948
Universal Military Training and Service Act, because it conditioned his exemption as a conscientious objector by whether
or not he believed in a "Supreme Being." Justice Clark concluded that Congress meant the phrase to embrace all religion,
and to exclude only political, sociological, or philosophical
views. The test was "whether a given belief that is sincere and
meaningful occupies a place in the life of its possessor parallel
to that filled by the orthodox belief in God of one who clearly
qualifies for the exemption." The task of administrative boards
was therefore "to decide whether the beliefs possessed by the
registrant are sincerely held and whether they are, in his own
scheme of things, religious."[39]

But what of someone who refused to characterize his beliefs
as "religious," yet nevertheless claimed status as a conscientious objector? This was the question in the most important
of all religion definition cases, *Welsh* v. *United States*, decided
in 1970. When Elliott Welsh registered for the draft he had
crossed out the world "religious" before he signed the conscientious objection form and he had also marked the form
"No" in response to the question on whether he believed in a
Supreme Being. Nevertheless, Justice Black's plurality opinion
in the case concluded that Welsh was not excluded from the
religious exemption. For the concept of "religion" had to be
broad enough to include "strong beliefs about our domestic
and foreign affairs or even . . . conscientious objection to participation in all wars . . . founded to a substantial extent upon
consideration of public policy." Only those would be excluded

"whose beliefs were not deeply held and those whose objection to war does not rest at all on moral, ethical or religious principle but instead rests solely upon consideration of policy, pragmatism, or expediency."[40]

Black's words are so important because his definition of religion avoids the conceptual problem hidden in the *Seeger* opinion: the nonviable distinction between a sincerely held religious belief and its moral or ethical counterpart. With such a definition administrative boards no longer need rely on some litmus test to distinguish the "really religious" from the "merely moral,"since the religious conscience and the moral conscience are one and the same and cannot be compartmentalized. The *Welsh* opinion also deletes any substantive requirement from religious belief (which *Seeger* required), so that there is no longer need to balance the "religious" and "secular" elements of an individual's beliefs in order to characterize them as either substantially "religious" or "essentially political, sociological, or philosophical." "Religion" for Black meant "conscience," which was originally its meaning for Madison when he wrote the Amendment's first draft. Madison regarded the terms as synonymous, and in debates over the Bill of Rights he freely substituted the one for the other.[41] Black's inclusion of the ethical and moral conscience within the statutory protection of religion was therefore quite traditional.

Supreme Court efforts to spell out the meaning of our nation's commitment to religious freedom have, then, tended to focus upon protection of the individual to act in conscience on the basis of his most deeply held beliefs. The religion clauses guarantee that such freedom of conscience is privileged, and that its exercise is not only to be encouraged, but may even be positively promoted by government. Exemption for the conscientious objector to all war is one example of such government "benevolence" toward religious freedom, an accommodation of Congress' power to raise armies with its recognition of the importance of free exercise values. The Court has never held that such a recognition is a promotion of religious belief, something which would violate the Establishment Clause. For " 'neutrality' in matters of religion is not inconsistent with 'benevolence' by way of exemption from onerous duties, so long as the exemption is tailored broadly enough that it reflects valid secular purposes."[42] This juxtaposition of the words

"neutrality" and "benevolence" in the context of the promotion of religious freedom demands some further clarification,
and this will be the aim of part three of this chapter.

III

American commitment to government neutrality in the area
of religion involves a paradox which has been well illustrated
in the conscientious objector cases just considered. Allowing
Congress to exempt the conscientious objector, however, merely
tells us clearly that a line exists between benevolence toward
religious freedom, which is permissible, and the advancement
of religion, which is not. We still do not know what the line
is; we only know where it is located in the case of draft exemption. The reason is that the concept of separation (whether
by line or wall) does not provide its own principle of limitation. Church-state separation (or neutrality) is not an absolute
but an instrumental principle. Its purpose is to promote and
support our nation's commitment to religious freedom, and
it is defensible only so long as it does so. The question therefore
is not whether there should be separation, but what its meaning should be in a given situation. Everyone is agreed that the
public care of religion is limited to care for freedom of conscience and religious association, as well as care for the internal autonomy of the churches. But when will these limits be
transgressed in one or other direction? The court's cases, Justice
Brennan once said, show "how elusive is the line which enforces the Amendment's injunction of strict neutrality, while
maintaining no hostility toward religion. . . . Inevitably, insistence upon neutrality . . . may appear to border upon religious hostility."[43] The principle of neutrality, in other words,
is not self-elucidating. The meaning of the concept (and our
commitment to it as a nation) has to be drawn from Supreme
Court decisions, rather than the meaning of the decisions from
the concept. Unless we have a Court decision in regard to a
specific government action, therefore, there is simply no way
to know a priori whether an action is in fact neutral toward
religion, and constitutes neither sponsorship nor interference.
The government may decide to locate the line of separation
at one or other point for purposes of a particular piece of legisla-

tion, but only the Court can say whether or not the line has been properly located.

The Court's first judgment on the line's location came in the famous *Everson* decision of 1947.[44] In discussing the religion clauses in the context of school busing, Justice Black stated that the Establishment Clause forbade funding and the Free Exercise Clause forbade discrimination. Government could not fund religious education, but neither could it deny public welfare benefits to Catholics who send their children to parochial schools. Busing, however, was neither a funding problem nor a discrimination problem; it fell into a third category of "permissible" public welfare benefits. The state could, but did not have to, provide safe transportation for all school children. Black's third category, permissible but not mandatory public services, was the Court's first effort to explain its neutrality ideal, and it thereby laid the foundation for the permissibility of many types of auxiliary services for children attending parochial schools. What Black did not do was to give any norms for deciding when a particular state "service" fell within one or other category. A year after *Everson* a majority of the Court decided that the use of public school property for religious instruction constituted impermissible aid to religion,[45] while in 1952 another majority decided that releasing children for religious instruction away from school property did not constitute aid.[46] Clearer norms were obviously needed, yet it was to take many years to elaborate them.

The 1963 *Schempp* case reaffirmed the neutrality principle: neither a state nor the federal government "can pass laws which aid one religion, aid all religions, or prefer one religion to another." The Court then went on to formulate a more precise test: *"What are the purpose and primary effect of the enactment?* If either is the advancement or inhibition of religion then the enactment exceeds the scope of legislative power." For a practice to be neutral, *"there must be a secular legislative purpose and a primary effect that neither advances nor inhibits religion."*[47] Applying this standard to devotional Bible reading and prayer in public schools, the Court found that these practices had more than a merely secular purpose, and sought an effect which clearly advanced religion. The same standard was used by the Court in 1968 to find a valid secular purpose for a New York law requiring local school districts to loan textbooks to private school students (namely, the furthering of educational opportunities for the young) as well as a neutral primary effect (providing financial benefits to parents by loaning free books to their children).[48]

In the 1970s this *Schempp* test was further refined by a third test for neutrality: the religion clauses also sought to avoid an excessive "entanglement" between the state and its agencies on the one hand, and religious bodies on the other. This test was developed by Chief Justice Burger, who then applied all three tests to permit property tax exemption for churches (a subject to be considered shortly),[49] as well as construction grants for private colleges and universities,[50] but not to permit support for the "secular teaching" done in parochial schools.[51] Gradually "primary effect" came to mean the "direct and immediate effect" of advancing or inhibiting religion. This modification was used in 1973 to invalidate New York grants for maintenance repairs to non-public schools and for tuition reimbursement to low-income parents.[52] It was used again in 1977, when a divided Court held that lending geography books to parochial school pupils did not violate neutrality, nor did therapeutic and diagnostic tests (because they concerned student health and were administered away from the school). But lending instructional materials like maps to the teacher was not neutral, said the Court, nor was sending public school teachers into parochial schools to teach remedial writing, reading, and arithmetic (since this was direct and immediate aid).[53]

In 1983 an important school tax case, *Mueller* v. *Allen*, held constitutional a 28-year-old Minnesota statute that allows taxpayers to deduct from their state income tax the expense of tuition, textbooks, and transportation of dependents who attend any elementary or secondary school. Writing for the narrow 5 to 4 majority, Justice Rehnquist emphasized that, unlike the tuition tax benefits in the 1973 New York case just mentioned, the deduction in the Minnesota statute is available to parents with children in either public or private schools: "a program . . . that neutrally provides state assistance to a broad spectrum of citizens is not readily subject to challenge under the Establishment Clause." He emphasized that a "state's decison to defray the cost of educational expenses incurred by parents—regardless of the type of schools their children attend—evidences a purpose that is both secular and understandable. . . . The historic purposes of the Clause simply do not encompass the sort of attenuated financial benefit, ultimately controlled by the private choices of individual parents, that eventually flows to parochial schools from the neutrally available tax benefit at issue in this case."[54] Moreover, added Rehnquist, an "essential feature" of the Minnesota tax deduction is that it is only one of many deductions in the law, such as those for medical expenses and charitable contributions.

In all these cases there is an obvious concern on the part of the Court to elaborate truly neutral standards of decision. But there is also a recurrent worry that some decisions will be interpreted as manifestations not of neutrality but of hostility. Thus Justice Douglas went out of his way in an early establishment case to underline the Court's duty to avoid any such hostility. "We are a religious people," he said, "whose institutions presuppose a Supreme Being. . . . When the state encourages religious instruction or cooperates with religious authorities by adjusting the schedule of public events to sectarian needs, it follows the best of our traditions. For it then respects the religious nature of our people and accommodates the public service to their spiritual needs. To hold that it may not would be to find in the Constitution a requirement that the government show a callous indifference to religious groups. . . . But we find no constitutional requirement which makes it necessary for government to be hostile to religion and to throw its weight against efforts to widen the effective scope of religious influence."[55] Justice Black was just as anxious that a 1962 Court decision should not seem to some "to indicate a hostility toward religion or toward prayer. Nothing, of course, could be more wrong. . . . It is neither sacrilegious nor antireligious to say that each separate government in this country should stay out of the business of writing or sanctioning official prayers and leave that purely religious function to the people themselves and to those the people choose to look to for religious guidance."[56]

The very next year Justice Clark felt compelled to defend the Court's decision in *Schempp* against the charge that, unless prayer and Bible reading are permitted in public schools, a "religion of secularism" would become established. "Nothing we have said here indicates that . . . study of the Bible or religion, when presented objectively as part of a secular program of education, may not be effected consistently with the First Amendment." Indeed, "it might well be said that one's education is not complete without a study of comparative religion or of the history of religion and its relationship to the advancement of civilization."[57] In the same opinion Justice Brennan spoke of "the Establishment Clause as a co-guarantor, with the Free Exercise Clause, of religious liberty," and emphasized that "forms of accommodation will reveal that the First Amendment commands not official hostility toward religion, but only a strict neutrality in matters of religion."[58] Several years later, in 1971, Chief Justice Burger felt compelled to give the same assurance after deciding against support of "secular teaching" in parochial schools: "Finally, nothing we have said can be construed to disparage the role of church-related elementary and secondary schools in our national life. Their contribution has been enormous. Nor do we ignore their economic plight in a period of rising cost and expanding need. . . . The sole question is whether state aid to these schools can be squared with the dictates of the Religion Clauses."[59]

The Court again underlined the importance of avoiding any government hostility toward religion in a 1983 case, *Marsh* v. *Chambers*. There the Court ruled, 6 to 3, that the Constitution permits a legislature, whether federal or state, to pay a chaplain to open each day's session with a prayer. "The opening of sessions of legislative and other deliberative public bodies with prayer," Chief Justice Burger wrote, "is deeply embedded in the history and tradition of this country," and "has become part of the fabric of our society." Burger noted that the lower courts had taken an unduly rigid view of the Establishment Clause. "To invoke Divine guidance on a public body entrusted with making the laws is not, in these circumstances, an 'establishment' of religion," he said, but "simply a tolerable acknowledgement of beliefs widely held among the people of this country." After reviewing the history of legislative prayer in the United States, Burger concluded that "the men who wrote the First Amendment Religion Clause did not view paid legislative chaplains and opening prayers as a violation of that Amendment, for the practice of opening sessions with prayers has continued without interruption ever since that early session of Congress."[60]

Official government promotion of prayer in public schools, however, was quite a different matter. In 1978 the Alabama legislature authorized a one minute period of silence in all public schools "for meditation," and three years later amended this by adding "or voluntary prayer." Twenty-five states now have such "minute of silence" statutes, and many explicitly say that students may meditate, pray, or reflect during this time. When the challenge to the Alabama statute was decided in 1985, Justice Stevens, writing for the 6-3 majority, said that offering students such opportunities for voluntary silent prayer does not violate the Establishment Clause. For such moments are not in themselves inherently religious (as Justice O'Connor noted in her concurring opinion), nor do pupils who participate in them need to compromise any of their beliefs. The Alabama statute, however, by adding "or voluntary prayer," demonstrated, said Stevens, that its "sole purpose" was to foster religious activity in the classroom and to "characterize prayer as a favored practice. Such an endorsement is inconsistent with the established principle that the government must pursue a course of complete neutrality toward religion." Stevens stressed the total absence of any secular purpose in the legislative history and the "wholly religious character" of the statute itself. "The legislative intent to return prayer to the public schools," he concluded, "is, of course, quite different from merely protecting every student's right to engage in voluntary prayer during an appropriate moment of silence during the school day."[61] Hence religious freedom can be sufficiently accommodated without the enactment of state laws explicitly promoting prayer in the classroom.

This concern of the Justices that neither Court nor government be hostile, or even indifferent, toward religion is the reason that one type of neutrality has never been acceptable to them. This is the type usually labeled "strict," as opposed to "benevolent" neutrality. As a theory it was first articulated in 1961 by Philip B. Kurland of the University of Chicago.[62] It proposed that the government simply not use religion as a basis for classification for purposes of any government action, whether that action be the conferring of rights or privileges or the imposition of obligations. Religion could be neither protected nor hindered by any statute. In the establishment area this would mean that any religious institution was eligible for participation in any governmental program which was not specifically designed to advantage religion. The government could in no way limit the religious character of participating schools, for this would be using religion as a basis for classification. In the free-exercise area, religiously motivated behavior would be protected only when government specifically legislated against it. Legislatures could thus regulate citizen behavior to further any otherwise proper objective, and religious belief would not be a ground for exemption from such regulation. Only if the regulation were directly aimed at a religious exercise would a First Amendment question arise, because then religion would be used as the basis of classification. This theory has been advocated on the Supreme Court only by Justice Harlan, who believed that no religious classification could be constitutional and that any benefits given by government to individuals should be "religion-blind." His principle was that of Kurland: "Neutrality . . . is a short form for saying that the government must neither legislate to accord benefits that favor religion over non-religion, . . . nor work deterrence of any religious belief."[63]

The reasons that the Court has not espoused this clear and straightforward interpretation of the religion clauses have been best explained by Chief Justice Burger in the important 1970 case, *Walz* v. *Tax Commission*. I already cited this opinion to illustrate the Court's flexibility in interpreting the religion clauses.[64] Burger there opted for an interpretation of neutrality which he called "benevolent," a word already used by Justice Clark and Justice Brennan in *Schempp*, and by Justice Brennan again in *Sherbert*.[65] This involved an acknowledgement that the religion clauses themselves suggest an inevitable intersection of church and state in certain areas, that "no perfect or absolute separation is really possible," and that some "room for play in the joints" had to be allowed. A government relationship with some religious activity would violate "benevolent" neutrality only when there was both sponsorship and active involvement.[66] Short of this, *some* government concern for religion is permissible. Religion, in other words, is not an invalid classification, but may sometimes be used to accommodate various segments of the population, provided that it is broad enough to include the most heterodox of believers. The judicial function is precisely to decide whether in a particular case religion may indeed be so used in order to strike a balance between the free-exercise and the establishment limitations. "The Court has struggled to find a neutral course between the two Religion Clauses both of which are cast in absolute terms, and either of which, if expanded to a logical extreme, would tend to clash with the other."[67]

"Benevolent neutrality" thus presumes that the balance between the clauses in any given instance must be *found*. "Strict neutrality," in contrast, presumes that the First Amendment has already struck the balance by eliminating religion altogether as a classification factor. The former approach allows wide latitude for legislative discretion vis-à-vis religion, while the latter precludes the very mention of religion in legislative judgements.[68] The former also remains open to the theory, advocated by a number of legal historians, that the two religion clauses were designated not so much to seal off the state from religious encroachment as to protect and promote religious liberty, as long as this did not overly involve the government with religion.[69] Ironically enough, even Justice Harlan had to concede that there are "too many areas in which the pervasive activities of the State justify some special provision for religion to prevent it from being submerged by an all-embracing secularism." From which he concluded that neutrality "is not so narrow a channel that the slightest deviation from an absolutely straight course leads to condemnation."[70] And he also concurred with Justice Goldberg's observation in *Schempp* that "untutored devotion to the concept of neutrality can lead to invocation or approval of results which partake . . . of a brooding and passive devotion to the secular and a passive or even active, hostility to religion."[71]

This clarification of benevolent neutrality was part of Chief Justice Burger's effort to explain in *Walz* why traditional property tax exemptions for churches are constitutional. These exemptions have been allowed throughout our history and have gone virtually unchallenged until recent years.[72] The challenge in this case came from Frederick Walz, who argued that exemption of church-owned property in New York City had the effect of raising his taxes and forcing him to contribute to an establishment of religion. Burger acknowledged that the effect of the exemption was clearly an indirect economic benefit to religious institutions, but he insisted that government involvement with religion, by allowing the exemption, was minimal and remote. Involvement would actually be far greater if all church property in the country had to be valued and taxed. Exemption thus passed the "excessive entanglement" test for neutrality, which was one of degree and duration, as we noted earlier.[73] "Separation in this context cannot mean the absence of all contact." The long history of the practice, moreover, showed that it has not in fact been the first in a series of steps leading toward establishment. Justice Holmes's observation should therefore be heeded; something practiced by common consent for two hundred years ought not to be overturned lightly.[74]

Burger's more interesting illumination of benevolent neutrality, however, came in his discussion of purpose rather than effect; what legitimate motivation could there be to exempt churches from taxation? Sponsorship (by direct subsidy) would clearly be illegitimate, and was also clearly not the case in tax exemption, since "government does not transfer part of its revenue to churches, but simply abstains from demanding that the church support the state."[75] Another purpose must also be ruled out: the giving of a reward to churches for specified public services. Burger's reasoning again relied upon his "excessive entanglement" test:

> We find it unnecessary to justify tax exemption on the social welfare services or "good works" that some churches perform for parishioners and others—family counselling, aid to the elderly and the infirm, and to children. Churches vary substantially in the scope of such services: programs expand or contract according to need. . . . The extent of social services may vary, depending on whether the church serves an urban or rural, a rich or poor constituency. To give emphasis to so variable an aspect of the work of religious bodies would introduce an element of governmental evaluation and standards as to the worth of a particular social welfare program, thus producing a kind of continuing day to day relationship which the policy of neutrality seeks to minimize. Hence, the use of a social welfare yardstick as a significant element to qualify for tax exemption could conceivably give rise to confrontations that could escalate to constitutional dimensions.[76]

This rejection of the "public service" purpose is obviously not an assertion that benefit to society is not a good secular justification for the enjoyment of special status by the churches, but only a denial that government is able to determine whether a given church is actually fulfilling its public function.[77] Only its members can determine that. It is they who must support their church. When and if they cease to do so, government has no right to keep it going.

The legitimate purpose of tax exemption, said Burger, was to "accommodate" religion, by including churches "within a broad class of property owned by non-profit, quasi-public corporations." Such accommodation neither interfered with religion in a way forbidden by the Free Exercise Clause, nor sponsored it in violation of the Establishment Clause. In short, it was neutral. In regard to exemption generally, however, the Court added: "Qualification for tax exemption is not perpetual or immutable; some tax exempt groups lose that status when their activities take them outside the classification and new entities can come into being and qualify for exemption."[78] Was Burger here applying to churches (along with other voluntary nonprofit organizations) the common precept of hornbook law that tax exemption is a privilege extended by legislative grace?[79]

Burger seemed to confirm this in the 8 to 1 majority opinion which he wrote in a 1983 tax case, which ruled that Bob Jones University and Goldsboro Christian Schools could not maintain their tax exempt status while holding policies that discriminate on the basis of race, even if those policies were based on sincerely held religious beliefs. Tax exemptions, he argued, were "justified on the basis that the exempt entity confers a public benefit—a benefit which the society or the community may not itself choose or be able to provide." Hence Congress intended that to qualify as charitable, organizations "must demonstrably serve and be in harmony with the public interest." Hence in this case the religious interest in discriminatory school policies must give way to the government's "compelling" interest in eliminating discrimination.[80]

Perhaps the strongest assertion of this "accommodation" principle came in the Court's 1984 establishment case, *Lynch* v. *Donnelly*. The city of Pawtucket, Rhode Island, had for some forty years erected and maintained a Nativity scene as part of its annual downtown Christmas display in a privately owned park in Pawtucket's business district. In 1980 Daniel Donnelly and other members of the local affiliate of the American Civil Liberties Union sued Mayor Dennis Lynch for violating the Establishment Clause. The District Court and the First Circuit Court of Appeals both held that, because erecting the Nativity scene had no secular purpose and had as its primary effect the advancement of religion, the Establishment Clause had been violated. The Supreme Court reversed these decisions in a 5 to 4 opinion written by Chief Justice Burger. His preliminary remarks are worth quoting at length:

No significant segment of our society and no institution within it can exist in a vacuum or in total or absolute isolation from all the other parts, much less from government. . . . Nor does the Consititution require complete separation of church and state; it affirmatively mandates accommodation, not merely tolerance, of all religions, and forbids hostility toward any. . . . There is an unbroken history of official acknowledgement by all three branches of government of the role of religion in American life from at least 1789. . . . This history may help explain why the Court consistently has declined to take a rigid, absolutist view of the Establishment Clause. . . .

Rather than mechanically invalidating all governmental conduct or statutes that confer benefits or given special recognition to religion in general or to one faith—as an absolutist approach would dictate—the Court has scrutinized challenged legislation or official conduct to determine whether, in reality, it establishes a religion or religious faith, or tends to do so. . . . In each case, the inquiry calls for line-drawing; no fixed, *per se* rule can be framed. . . . In the line-drawing process we have often found it useful to inquire whether the challenged law or conduct has a secular purpose, whether its principle or primary effect is to advance or inhibit religion, and whether it creates an excessive entanglement of government with religion. . . . But, we have repeatedly emphasized our unwillingness to be confined to any single test or criterion in this sensitive area.[81]

Burger then concluded that, in the Pawtucket case, whatever benefit the Nativity scene was to one faith or religion or to all religions, this was indirect, remote and incidental: "display of the crèche is no more an advancement or endorsement of religion than the Congressional and Executive recognition of the origins of the Holiday itself as 'Christ's Mass,' or the exhibition of literally hundreds of religious paintings in governmentally supported museums." The city also clearly had a secular purpose for the inclusion of this religious symbol with all the other figures and decorations associated with Christmas, namely to engender "a friendly community spirit of good will in keeping with the season. . . . Any notion that these symbols pose a real danger of establishment of a state church is far-fetched indeed."[82] Hence Government does not violate the Establishment Clause by officially recognizing the role of religion in American life, not even when this recognition includes a specific acknowledgement of the Christian origin of Christmas. The Chief Justice emphasized that the Nativity scene was passive: by displaying it Government was trying neither to preach nor to worship, but simply to join in the celebration.

Before we close this discussion of the "overlap of the two religion clauses" (to use Justice Clark's phrase in *Schempp*),[83] we should note one other instance: the chaplaincy program in the armed services. A rigid separationist position would mean the elimination of this program. Yet in spite of the fact that such elimination would have the great advantage of relieving the military of some highly embarrassing problems involving the establishment of religious categories and the apportionment of facilities, it has never been seriously advocated. This is not because the impartial aid to religion involved in the chaplaincy program is thought to be an appropriate object of government. The reason is rather that insistence upon "strict separation" in this area would limit religious freedom and so violate neutrality. For as Justice Clark noted in *Schempp*, in military service "Government regulates the temporal and geographic environment of individuals to a point that, unless it permits voluntary religious services to be conducted with the use of government facilities, military personnel would be unable to engage in the practice of their faiths."[84] Here again, then, it is clear that the root aim of government neutrality is to maximize religious freedom, and only that degree of separation is required which is compatible with such freedom.[85]

IV

I would like to conclude this chapter by highlighting what would seem at first glance to be the one large anomaly in the Court's search for the best ways to be neutral toward religion, namely the difference between charitable and educational institutions with respect to the constitutionality of financial assistance by the government. Federal and state governments routinely fund church-related hospitals, orphanages, old age and nursing homes, but with church-related schools nothing has been routine. Indeed, these schools have become the single greatest symbol of the separation of church and state in America, one that pervasively affects the whole fabric of our society. The reasons for this obviously do not lie in the concept of separation itself, since other nations that have separated church and state find no difficulty at all in providing nondiscriminatory aid to all church-related schools.[86] Many American jurists have argued, moreover, that such public funding would be a means of promoting, not religion, but precisely religious freedom, that is to say, the freedom of religious choice. For the burden of sharing the enormous cost of public education, properly assessed upon all taxpayers, greatly reduces the practical freedom to choose a school not supported by public funds. Not to lift this restraint, so the argument goes, is to discriminate against religious schools precisely because they are religious, thereby greatly weakening the force of the Free Exercise Clause.[87]

The only Justice sympathetic with this line of argument has been Byron White. In his 1971 dissent in *Lemon* v. *Kurtzman*[88] White noted the Court's general recognition that in American society parochial schools perform both religious and secular functions. Prior cases had also recognized, he continued, referring to his own opinion for the Court in *Allen*,[89] that legislation having a secular purpose, and extending government assistance to sectarian schools in the performance of these secular functions, does not constitute an "establishment of religion" merely because the secular program may incidentally benefit a church in fulfilling its religious mission. "The Establishment Clause, however, coexists in the First Amendment with the Free Exercise Clause and the latter is surely relevant in cases such as these. Where a state program seeks to insure the proper education of its young, in private as well as public schools, free exercise considerations at least counsel against refusing support for students attending parochial schools simply because in that setting they are also being instructed in the tenets of the faith they are constitutionally free to practice."[90]

White then put his finger upon the root reason for a consistent refusal to allow public funding of parochial schools: the conviction of the majority of the Justices that in practice it really would be impossible to distinguish in any principled way the promotion of religious freedom on this elementary school level from the promotion of religious belief. This was quite clear in the *Lemon* case, because in that record there was no evidence at all that teachers participating in the Rhode Island salary-supplement program had injected religion into any of their secular subjects—in fact the District Court had positively found that they had not. The Supreme Court, however, as White recognized, was not concerned with actualities but with potentialities: the possibility that religion *could* be fostered in classrooms supported by state funds, and the likelihood that any effort to see to it that religion was *not* fostered, would lead to too much state "entanglement" with the religious institutions. "The Court thus creates an insoluble paradox for the State and the parochial schools. The State cannot finance secular instruction if it permits religion to be taught in the same classroom; but if it exacts a promise that religion not be taught—a promise the school and its teachers are quite willing and on this record able to give—and enforces it, it is then entangled in the 'no entanglement' aspect of the Court's Establishment Clause jurisprudence."[91]

In the same case Justice Douglas freely agreed with White that the Court was caught in a dilemma in regard to parochial schools. But he pointed out the overriding reason for its remaining caught, a reason White never mentioned: "If the government closed its eyes to the manner in which these grants are actually used it would be allowing public funds to promote sectarian education. If it did not close its eyes, but undertook the surveillance needed, it would, I fear, intermeddle in parochial affairs *in a way that would breed only rancor and dissension*."[92] Chief Justice Burger, who wrote the majority opinion in *Lemon*, spoke also of "the divisive political potential" of funding parochial schools, and emphasized that "political division along religious lines was one of the principal evils against which the First Amendment was intended to protect. . . . The potential divisiveness of such conflict is a threat to the normal political process. . . . To have States or communities divide on the issues presented by state aid to parochial schools would tend to confuse and obscure other issues of great urgency."[93] Indeed, the ultimate reason for the Court applying a different standard to funds for higher education (as Burger did in *Tilton*) is precisely the presence of factors which, in their cumulative impact, "substantially lessen the potential for divisive religious fragmentation in the political area."[94]

In other words, the Court has really developed a fourth test for neutrality, the avoidance of political strife, though it has been reluctant to label it as such.[95] This fourth test is what is in fact behind the apparently anomalous application of benevolent neutrality in the case of church-related elementary and secondary schools. The dangers are not constitutional but political. Nondiscriminatory aid to these schools could indeed be justified by the First Amendment if this Amendment were to be taken out of the context of life in modern America. Within this context, however, there is simply too much opposition to any "overlap" of church and state in the educational area. Schools have become, as I already mentioned, *the* symbol of the American ideal of church-state separation. It is almost as if there were some tacit agreement, by a very large segment of society, that if an absolutely strict separation should be maintained here, an impregnable wall built wide and high, then the ideal will be secure, and movable lines, "overlap" and accommodation may be more easily tolerated elsewhere, in order that our *other* American ideal of benevolence toward religion might also be secure.

Nowhere is this acute anxiety in the educational area about strict separation, "overlap," and movable lines better illustrated than in two 5-4 decisions in 1985, both involving instruction by full-time public school teachers on parochial school premises. The first case involved a state-funded program in Grand Rapids, Michigan, providing remedial and enrichment classes in mathematics, reading, and other subjects for about 11,000 children in 40 parochial schools. The city school system leased classes for $6.00 per classroom, requiring that each room be free of religious symbols and that a sign be posted stating that the room was a "public school classroom." The second case dealt with a New York City program, federally funded under Title I of the Elementary and Secondary Education Act of 1965, to provide remedial instruction for impoverished children. About 200,000 poor children were involved, 22,000 of whom were in parochial schools. New York had originally required parochial pupils to travel to public school buildings for release-time instruction. But experience showed that it was too difficult to draw pupils from one school to another, and so New York eventually decided to do what almost all Title I programs nationwide were doing, namely to send their teachers into parochial school buildings during regular class hours. As an extra protection, New York City supervisors periodically spot-checked the classrooms to insure that their instructors stayed clear of religious issues.

Justice Brennan wrote the majority opinion in both cases, joined by Justices Marshall, Powell, Blackmun, and Stevens. His efforts in each to draw a line that achieved an absolutely strict separation resulted in some rather strained argumentation. In the Grand Rapids case he quickly conceded that the program satisfied the first *Lemon* test, because it had the plainly secular purpose of educating children. But because 40 of the 41 private schools involved were religious, he concluded that the program failed the second *Lemon* test, because "it may impermissibly advance religion." Note that his use of "may" betrays that same fear of potentialities that both White and Burger recognized in their *Lemon* opinions. This fear was made more explicit in Brennan's list of the program's three dangers: the public school teachers may religiously indoctrinate students at public expense; the mere presence of these teachers on parochial school premises may ("at least in the eyes of impressionable youngsters") convey a message of state support of religion; the public funding involved may have the effect of subsidizing the religious mission of the schools by allowing them to offer secular subjects which they might otherwise have to fund themselves.

Under fire from dissenting Justices Rehnquist and O'Connor, Brennan admitted there was no evidence to substantiate the first danger, yet insisted that "the absence of proof of specific instances is not dispositive." Rehnquist and O'Connor might also have objected that the second danger is of its nature not susceptible to proof by concrete evidence. And Brennan's own words show how conjectural was the third reason: "there is no way of knowing whether the religious schools would have offered some or all of the courses if the public school curriculum had not offered them first." His opinion ended with a revealing statement: "To let the genie out of the bottle in this case would be to permit even larger segments of the religious school curriculum to be turned over to the public school system."[96]

In the New York case, on the other hand, Brennan bypassed the first two *Lemon* tests entirely, focusing exclusively on the efforts of supervisors to insure that the first two tests were satisfied. This, said Brennan, clearly constituted entanglement and so failed the third *Lemon* test—leaving New York officials in what dissenting Justice Rehnquist called a "Catch-22": aid must be supervised to ensure no entanglement but supervision itself is held to cause such entanglement. Brennan even sought to defend religious schools against intrusion by Government agents (as if the schools were among the plaintiffs), arguing that they "must obey these same agents" and "must endure the ongoing presence of state personnel." While the Court's ruling did not affect Title I and its provisions (federal monies still had to be spent equally for public and private school pupils in poor neighborhoods), it did affect disadvantaged children in cities where remedial classes adjacent to parochial schools were not economically or logistically feasible.

In her dissent Justice O'Connor pointed out that there were more than 20,000 of such disadvantaged children in New York City alone and uncounted others elsewhere. "For these children," she said, "the Court's decision is tragic," for it deprives them of a program that offers a meaningful chance of success in life, and it does so on the untenable theory that the public school teachers are likely to start teaching religion merely because they have walked across the threshold of a parochial school."[97] The ruling also had a more bizarre consequence: cities throughout the country were suddenly trying to find ways to get as close as possible to this threshold without actually going in. Boston, Chicago, New York, Philadelphia, and Los Angeles decided to try teaching children in mobile trailers parked on the sidewalk next to the schools, to use public libraries and parks nearby, or to put public school teachers on closed circuit television. City officials were meanwhile expressing an understandable puzzlement that, after twenty years without the slightest civic unrest, the line of separation between church and state now had to be drawn at the schoolhouse door.[98]

These two 1985 decisions obviously satisfied the secularists in America who favor a very strict neutrality and oppose all accommodation to religion. They quite understandably resent the use of tax monies for any support at all of religious activities, however indirect, because they believe that their value system provides just as strong a basis for loyalty to their country as belief in a Supreme Being. They consequently experience government benevolence toward religion in any form as pressure upon themselves, as an assertion of something they vehemently deny, namely that religion is good for society and necessary for the well-being of the republic. Protestant and Jewish groups, of which I spoke at the start, would not, of course, share this opposition of the secularists to all government benevolence toward religion. Nevertheless, they want very strict separation in the educational area because they believe, again quite understandably, that nondiscriminatory aid to religious schools would inevitably discriminate in its allocation in favor of the large Catholic school system, something which seems to them neither honestly neutral nor basically just. It is this conviction of a large segment of American society, both secular and sectarian, that any type of support to religious schools would be unfair to *them*, which is the basis for that potential for political division along religious lines which the Supreme Court seeks to avoid. For significant sums of money would be involved in such support, and it is indeed unlikely that the year to year legislative bargaining and voting for such money could ever produce even a tolerable level of satisfaction among the participants.

Thus the Court's interpretation of government neutrality toward religion in the educational area is not as anomalous as it might at first seem, but is rather based upon a clear value choice. Some limited cooperation between church and state may well be as possible in the educational area as in any other area, insofar as the aim of such cooperation is the promotion of religious freedom. But in no case can the result of such benevolence become a potential for serious and open conflict in the body politic. Paul Freund has admirably summed up this value choice: "Although great issues of constitutional law are never settled until they are settled right, still as between open-ended, on-going political warfare and such binding quality as judicial decisions possess, I would choose the latter in the field of God and Caesar and the public treasury."[99]

Were the Court to proceed otherwise, allowing the political process to function freely and permitting government to be benevolent in the educational area, they would then be opposing the values of a highly articulate constituency representing the majority of American citizens, and they would be doing so in an area where history is at best cloudy and precedent slim. Richard Morgan has well summarized their situation: "The Supreme Court may be able, indeed, it may be one of its important functions, to set the pace of national policy change from time to time. But there are limits. For the Court to attempt to swim across powerfully moving tides in search of doctrinal consistency would be to risk the long-run political position of the institution just as surely as continued slighting of the value of doctrinal consistency would risk that position. Constitutional 'principles' are meaningless unless the values they are meant to serve are made explicit, and the whole attempt is bootless if the values are not widely shared."[100] In other words, in the educational area the line separating the promotion of religious belief from the promotion of religious freedom is going to remain rather jagged for some time to come.

3

Public Morality and Law

We take for granted in our Western tradition a certain convergence between morals and law. Morality, insofar as it applies to our public lives, is assumed to follow legality. We believe that in normal social circumstances we can recognize the moral values of a nation in its laws. We therefore reject any suggestion that there can be such things as amoral politics or unpolitical morality. We assert that the fundamental moral principle in politics ought to be the observance of our country's legal processes, since legal process ought to coincide with moral conviction. When this is not the case, we insist, when there is no assimilation into the political arena of the moral convictions behind our laws, then the laws themselves will lose respect and we shall have more Watergates and worse.[1]

In this chapter I would like to look more closely at this conviction of ours that the legal standard is the moral standard for politics and government. I would like to make three affirmations about law as a standard for public morality: first, it is a minimum standard; second, minimum though it is, law is nonetheless a necessary standard; third, because it is both minimum and necessary, law as a standard is therefore incomplete.

I

To understand, first of all, why law ought to be a minimum standard for public morality, we have to recognize as quite distinct the two areas of morals and public policy. Morality and law may be intimately related, but they are not identical. Not everything which is outside the strictures of the penal code is morally permissible; neither should everything that is morally wrong be made criminal. Morality governs the totality of human behavior, both personal and social. All aspects of our freedom come under its ken, even our most intimate thoughts, desires, and motivations. Law, on the other hand, looks only to visible behavior. It reaches only those aspects of our freedom which are formally social. It is also by its nature coercive, and, because men and women can be coerced into moral action only to a very limited extent, the moral scope of society's laws can never be very extensive.[2] In other words, the moral aspirations of law ought to be minimal.

This does not mean that city, state, and federal legislatures, in making laws, may not look to the moral good of society. They should. But they must recognize that laws should not deal with everything that is morally desirable. Obviously a given community or nation can reach consensus on some social duty, and as a consequence enact laws that regulate behavior and nurture certain moral values. In this sense government does at times "legislate morality." But a law reflecting high moral ideals that will not be obeyed by the majority of citizens, is bad as law, because no means is a good means unless it works well in most cases. Likewise a law which is unenforceable, or whose enforcement has harmful effects in other areas of social life, is likely to defeat its own aims and eventually bring itself into contempt. When faced with what it considers a social evil, therefore, a legislature must ask whether coercive law is the best means to eradicate it. It may be that law will have to be tolerant of this particular vice which morality condemns, leaving its alleviation to other institutions, such as church, home, school, or civic organizations, all of which are concerned with the maintenance of moral standards. The question for both electorate and legislature is thus not whether it believes a given action to be immoral, but whether it believes such action should be punished by law.

Indeed, as John Courtney Murray once observed, the greater a particular social evil is thought to be, the less effective against it may be the instrument of coercive law.[3] No society, for example, can expect very much in the way of moral uplift from its censorship laws, unless these express what is already the community's conviction and outrage. Laws may indeed proscribe pornography, but insofar as this becomes a pervasive and generally accepted social phenomenon, as it seems to have become in the United States, the power of police against it is severely limited. To acknowledge this fact is not to make a moral judgment that allowing pornography is *better* than banning it, but only a tactical judgment that banning it by law is not the best means to proceed against it. The alternative to this understanding of good law, namely as an expression of community conviction regarding what is moral and what is not, is to enforce laws independent of general consensus. But this we have always understood to be tyranny.

The relation of law to three very different types of social problem will illustrate the point I am making here. The first is the pervasive racial discrimination that was tolerated in our society for generations, but which in the 1960s became morally intolerable to the majority of citizens. The result was the Civil Rights Act of 1964, by which Congress manifested the growing consensus that such discrimination was wrong and should be eliminated by law. The Act's enforcement over the last two decades has indeed "legislated morality" insofar as it has affected public behavior based upon a consensus of public morality. The very opposite phenomenon resulted from the enactment of laws dealing with Prohibition in the 1920s. These had little effect upon social behavior regarding the consumption of alcohol because there was no consensus at all that such public consumption was in itself morally wrong, a fact that eventually produced resentment by the majority of citizens that government should be forcing them by law to think so. The third social problem is the as yet unresolved question of abortion. Clearly this is a moral problem and clearly the matter is one of public morality, since it involves decisions regarding the rights of human fetuses, as well as the resolution of conflicts between such rights, if recognized, and the rights of privacy and personal freedom in situations experienced as oppressive and harmful to women. Genuine moral imperatives exist on the side of both sets of rights, and, because no national consensus has yet emerged, the conflict ought to remain in the public forum and not be prematurely resolved by government before its time.

Law thus reflects, but in no sense determines, the moral worth of a society. It is instrumental to national purpose and community instinct, and will be successful in mediating moral values insofar as these reflect such purpose and instinct. In the past decade, for example, forty-six of the fifty states have enacted new ethics legislation. These enactments will no doubt contain but will hardly solve the problem of corruption in politics. One reason is that history shows corruption to be largely endemic in the American system. Another more fundamental reason is that most of the new ethics codes are about money, while Watergate has shown us all that there is a much more insidious source of corruption than money.[4] Grant Gilmore's judgment is thus both eloquent and wise: law never has been, and never will be, the salvation of any society. "The values of a reasonably just society," he writes," will reflect themselves in a reasonably just law. The better the society, the less law there will be. In Heaven there will be no law, and the lion will lie down with the lamb. The values of an unjust society will reflect themselves in an unjust law. The worse the society, the more law there will be. In Hell there will be nothing but law, and due process will be meticulously observed."[5]

What we have said thus far about law as a minimum standard for public morality consequently raises a very serious question for American society: if our norm for whether laws that enforce morality are good or bad is their relation to community consensus on what is moral and what is not, how does this community go about reaching such consensus? We want to be a good people, but how shall we manage to agree on what "good" means in any given situation? We want to be a free people, but how shall we manage to agree on what to do with our freedom? In a pluralist society such as ours, the problem of popular consent to law and coercion thus becomes critical. For as a people we espouse different ideologies which inevitably lead to conflicts of moral values—basic religious differences, to name but one source. Often such conflicts are irreducible, because there is simply no single group of persons which can be agreed upon as the final arbiter of morality. Yet such conflicts, we have also come to believe, give rise to moral judgments which are as close to the practical truth as we can get. In other words, as a free people in a pluralist society, we accept the principle that conflict among all interested parties to a decision can be creative of moral insight.

This recognition of the positive value in public conflict is extremely important, and must be reaffirmed again and again. For there is a perennial temptation to see harmony as the ideal pattern in public relationships and an innate reluctance to seek the resolution of conflict through argument and compromise. Yet where such conflicts are hidden or denied instead of confronted, communities inevitably become paralyzed and stalemated. Such communities pay an enormous cost for this inaction, because intractable social problems and the turmoil of competing demands shake them much more deeply than conflicts which are worked through. Rising public disagreement should therefore be welcomed, not feared, as long as the parties to the dispute are committed to resolving the conflict and adjusting their prior claims in the light of the public argument. But if either party is so committed to one possible outcome that they are unwilling to consider any alternative, then of course the particular conflict cannot be creative at all, and no new possibilities for the community can be realized.[6]

James Madison believed that this management of conflict was the major end of government, and he and the other drafters wrote this philosophy into the United States Constitution. They all judged that power is enhanced, not diminished, by diffusing it throughout society rather than by concentrating it in one person or branch of government. Their system of checks and balances was a profound act of trust in the collective wisdom of the people and a positive evaluation of community conflict as a source of unity, progress, and public morality. We rediscovered the value of such constitutionalism in the wake of Watergate, during which we learned anew that political truth is arrived at by fostering conflict among the branches of government, and that without such conflict the truth will continue to escape us.

If we ask why such a positive evaluation of conflict in the public and political spheres has not brought chaos to American government, the answer lies in another conviction of the Founding Fathers, so obvious to them that they felt no need to incorporate it into the Constitution, namely that the pursuit of the common good was and would continue to be a major motivation of all citizens. This is what Jefferson meant when he said in the Declaration of Independence that we as a people believed one of our inalienable rights to be "the pursuit of happiness." For this phrase referred not just to individual happiness, but much more to what was commonly called, in the political literature of the time, "public happiness." The right to pursue public or social happiness was not the negative right of individuals to be protected by government *from* something; rather it was their positive right to be engaged *in* something, the right to pursue the public good in the public realm.[7] For the Founders such pursuit was the exercise of "public virtue."

Such public happiness, moreover, was not conceived of as something already in existence and therefore to be found, but as something to be created. Even though its pursuit was declared to be a natural right, that which was pursued was never thought to be natural at all, but rather the product of human imagination and public conflict. No superior judgment of some elite, much less that of any single person, can be presumed under this rationale to know a priori what in any given situation is valuable, wise, and just. One can only know this in a pluralist society through the creativity of conflicting minds grappling with a particular societal problem in search of the moral and the true. To channel such public argument, we as a nation indeed need law and legal principles, but these must at least be concerned with allowing conflicting moral imperatives to be argued orderly in the public forum. Law, in other words, should be used to mediate conflicts in public morality, not wielded like a bludgeon to resolve them before their time.[8]

II

What we have just said about "public happiness" will enable us to see more easily, I think, why law, even though it ought to constitute no more than a minimum standard for public morality, remains nonetheless a necessary standard. This is my second point, and it follows from the American belief that the free pursuit of competing individual and group interests will conduce to the common good. That is to say, such pursuit will produce a system that not only displays tolerable stability but also gives to each person a more or less equitable share of society's goods, roughly approximating our notions of distributive justice. However, action of this type by competing groups inevitably generates conflict (by changing the relative strength of individuals and groups), and this conflict in turn inevitably generates litigation. Hence no society which encourages competition, as does ours, can long survive as just and moral if the resulting conflicts are not regulated by law. When changing social practice demands new law, moreover, competing individual interests will see to it that suits are brought to reevaluate what is just and fair and, if necessary, furnish the basis for the enactment of new law.

It is a moot point, of course, whether these basic American

beliefs about competition and conflict also promote justice for those segments of society seldom involved in litigation. This is a separate question about which we shall speak later. My point here is simply that these public conflicts result in public regulation, and that such regulatory law is absolutely necessary. "Men are not devils dominated by a wish to exterminate each other," writes H. L. A. Hart. "But neither are they angels, and the fact that they are a mean between these two extremes is something which makes a system of mutual forbearances both necessary and possible. . . . Human altruism is limited in range and intermittent, and the tendencies to aggression are frequent enough to be fatal to social life if not controlled." Hence "what reason demands is voluntary cooperation in a coercive system. If a system of rules is to be imposed by force on any, there must be a sufficient number who accept it voluntarily. Without their voluntary cooperation, thus creating authority, the coercive power of law and government cannot be established."[9]

Law, then, is the institution which is seen by society as the embodiment of reason and order in the public domain. The precise yet inconclusive argument on affirmative action in the *Bakke* case, for example, or those arguments about why abortion is or is not unlike murder, or about the difference between killing and not prolonging life, are each an exercise of reason in the weighing of facts as well as in the creation of orderly procedures for the processing of facts. With law available as a medium, highly emotional issues of life and death need not be decided without the guidance of careful argument, even if the final legal outcome is not a conclusive proof but only a well reasoned opinion. What matters is that this legal outcome, whatever it might be in any given public policy, should manifest a systematic concern with justice. This is why the legal profession, like other professions, has always claimed to distinguish itself from nonprofessional occupations by justifying its activities in terms other than direct self-interest. It claims from society a certain respect and autonomy, and offers in return to develop its knowledge, to provide society with increased technical competence, and to avoid exploiting situations for the personal gain of its members.[10]

Law is also a necessary standard of public morality because so much law is involved in the behavior of those two groups which worry the public most: the management staff of large corporations and the top echelons of major government agencies. Their behavior is judged properly, though not exclusively, by whether it conforms to the law's requirements. This does not mean that business and government are mere instruments of their legal counsel. Other determinants are obviously more influential in their operation than legal advice. But almost all these determinants have significant legal components, such as antitrust laws, election contribution laws, the policies of regulatory agencies, and congressional statutes, to name only the more obvious. For in our century we have come to realize as a nation that power must be contained, not only in the political order but in the economic order as well. A study published in the *Harvard Business Review* found that half the 1,700 corporation executives polled agreed with the following statement: "The American business executive tends to ignore the great ethical laws as they apply immediately to his work. He is preoccupied chiefly with gain." Another survey, published in the *Wall Street Journal*, found that out of some 500 top and middle managers only 50 percent said that bribes should not be paid to foreign officials.[11] The focus of public morality, in other words, rests on business as well as government, and law is necessary to regulate both forms of power.

I have been considering law as necessary for regulating those conflicts in society which we as a people encourage. But law is also necessary as the means to defend our individual rights of life, liberty, and property. We have always believed these to be paramount, and are convinced as a nation that the "good" of our society consists in making them secure. Yet to secure one's rights by defense means that it is necessary not only to have law but also lawyers. At the beginning of this century there was one lawyer for every 1,100 Americans. We now have one for every 388. We have been and continue to be a litigious people, and our adversary or "fight" theory of justice, being a sort of legal laissez-faire, has inevitably led to more and more court actions to defend what individuals and groups believe to be their rights. Hence in discussing public morality in our country we must also ask about the morality of the more than 600,000 lawyers who presently do this defending in some form or other.

More particularly we ought to ask about the morality of that 10 percent of these 600,000 whose legal services are necessary for the smooth functioning of government and large corporations. For this group's concept of ethical responsibility has consequences out of all proportion to its size. Many of these lawyers have positions of great authority and influence, and are in turn models of legal counsel in the modern industrial system. Their particular ethical problems, moreover, exemplify problems which are encountered by all lawyers in the practice of their profession.[12] Yet the ethics of this elite group are constantly under suspicion. The public is generally anxious about them precisely because they serve powerful clients. The esteem in which they have always been held has therefore had its ambivalence: while we acknowledge the necessity of law to express our fundamental values of morality and justice, we often think of lawyers who practice within this "power structure" as somehow ignoring morality and perverting justice. We tend to transfer to them our current distrust of our institutions and of the people who hold special authority and power in them. "The weight of public responsibility falling on these elites has become heavier in proportion as the task of defining and resolving issues of community interest and welfare has increasingly devolved upon professional specialists."[13]

This recent public distrust of lawyers generally, and of influential lawyers in particular, is thus the negative side of recognizing their necessity in society. The practicing bar has reacted to this bad press by going through its own crisis of self-confidence. The American Bar Association, for example, has recently revised its 1969 Code of Professional Responsibility, that set off detailed administration regulations by which the legal profession monitors itself. Yet however necessary such a legal code may be as a prohibition against obviously immoral actions, it can do little to help the lawyer when he or she encounters a true moral problem in professional practice. When lawyers face genuine ethical dilemmas they have by definition already exhausted the limits of their technical judgment based on professional knowledge. They remain in doubt and continue in the dilemma precisely because they have found no help in the traditional negative prescriptions of the Code. At best these are only remotely useful, if not quite irrelevant to the realities of practice. Because the Code is largely prohibitive, it cannot possibly be pervasive. New and wholly unforeseen situations thus make the moral dimensions of law fully as complex as those technical labyrinths which lawyers are trained so well to negotiate.

It is therefore not at all surprising that many lawyers refuse to recognize moral dilemmas when confronted by them, or develop ways of rationalizing actions so as to avoid the dilemmas altogether. For to resolve such dilemmas the professional must put himself on the line intellectually and morally. He must say to himself and to others that he not only understands his proper role and responsibilities in a given situation, but that others must trust him in the type of action he chooses. These are strong statements, and the person who can make them presents in his own life a much stronger justification for the necessity of lawyers than that to which the public has become accustomed. For he is willing to deal with an ethical problem by putting something of his own identity on the line. In contrast, all that the Code of Professional Responsibility can do is to set limits on the range of permissible choices; no such code can give directions as to how much of oneself to put at risk on any single occasion. Ultimately the resolution of moral questions in law or any other profession is, as in everyday life itself, an act of self-creation.[14]

III

This nonprofessional, fundamentally human character of moral decision, of which we have just spoken, easily leads us now to consider how incomplete law must necessarily be as a standard for public morality. This follows in large part, as I said at the outset, from the fact that it is so necessary and yet so minimum. Consider for a moment Alexander Solzhenitsyn's remarks of Harvard University's 1978 Commencement:

> I have spent all my life under a Communist regime and I will tell you that a society without any objective legal scale is a terrible one indeed. But a society with no other scale but the legal one is not quite worthy of man either. The letter of the law is too cold and formal to have a beneficial influence on society. Whenever the tissue of life is woven of legalistic relations, there is an atmosphere of moral mediocrity, paralyzing man's noblest impulses.[15]

The danger, then, is to believe that, because law is necessary for the public weal, nothing else is necessary. If legality is the highest goal and nothing else is required, then everybody, as

Solzhenitsyn notes, is encouraged to operate "at the extreme limit of these legal frames. An oil company is legally blameless when it purchases an invention of a new type of energy to prevent its use. A food product manufacturer is legally blameless when he poisons his product to make it last longer; after all, people are free not to buy it." There must be, Solzhenitsyn continues, some higher and more important standard than the legal: "a society which is based on the letter of the law and never reaches any higher is scarcely taking advantage of the high level of human possibilities. . . . And it will simply be impossible to survive the trials of this threatening century with only the support of a legalistic structure."[16] Solzhenitsyn's own experience, of course, would not make him sympathetic with those traditional American experiences of compromise, self-doubt, and experiment. And one critic has observed that the Russian novelist may really believe that the cure for evil totalitarianism is good totalitarianism, in contrast to our own belief that what holds us together as a community is not homogeneity but diversity.[17] Be that as it may, this call of Solzhenitsyn's for America not to lose its spiritual bearings must be heard and taken seriously if we are not to give up all concern about public morality and government.

As I noted earlier, we do not in America use law to influence human behavior (and therefore to shape our inner lives and character) except to the minimum extent that such law reflects national consensus as to the common good. Our democratic system constitutes indeed a major negative insight into human character: we tolerate a number of competing ideas on the supposition that we are safer from tyranny when no one person or group can claim a right to all the power. No religious or political philosophy may be pushed at the expense of any other, for we know well the ugly results of attempting to enshrine one ideal by punishing all dissident religious or political views. The difficulty, however, is that we may neglect that most elementary yet crucial distinction between holding strong moral convictions and imposing them on others. The morality we enforce by law may and should be minimum, but if we think that there is no moral obligation other than the legal, then we are in trouble.[18] Even Madison, the architect of our system for restraining power, assumed that for such a system to work, there had to be virtuous people. Freedom, he realized, could not be maintained solely by skilled lawyers, principled judges, or competing politicians; if it did not engage the deepest sentiments of the people, and if these sentiments did not include high moral ideals, all would eventually be lost. Madison's point, however, is that the political system itself is not to be relied upon either to produce such virtuous people or to inculcate such ideals.[19]

This does not mean that creative political leadership cannot tap this virtue and direct these ideals by arousing a people's hopes and aspirations. Leaders, as opposed to mere power-wielders, can indeed mobilize the very best in their followers and activate their highest levels of personal motive and social morality. For morality, unlike ethical reflection, is not a purely rational phenomenon; it is also a product of affectivity, mysticism, and faith. Morality is usually learned at a parent's knee, through religious instruction, and from one's subculture and peer groups. Political leaders cannot create such moral conviction, but they can evoke and channel it; they can summon people to action and help them to choose what to do with their freedom. True leadership knows how to locate that value consensus in society which is the source of all law and which establishes those conditions in which legislation is able to promote the just society. But the wellsprings of morality itself are not located in the political order.

Our American system of government, then, with its commitment to tolerance and freedom of expression, really presupposes that citizens have tested their ideals and moral judgments before they speak or act, in order to judge for themselves whether they are true or false, good or bad. Pluralism does not mean that one idea is as good as any other, or that conflicting views of morals and truth are all equally valid. Rather it means that each idea and moral conviction is relevant if it is responsibly held by any citizen. This is the source of that public politeness and respect on the part of those who experience very different moral imperatives. Such civility is indeed a concrete expression of charity, by which Americans express genuine epistemological humility, and an unwillingness to cause pain in social manners and institutions.[20] But it does not follow that, for example, religious institutions need be any less zealous in asserting moral standards or in speaking out on public issues. For this is the way that churches summon us to live up to our ideals and place high value on those courses of action which benefit society as a whole. The point is simply that this bear-

ing of public moral witness is of an order very different from
that of civil law.

Let me make a final observation on this incompleteness
of law as a standard. Earlier I emphasized the necessity of
lawyers, but it is important to recognize also that lawyers
precisely as lawyers are severely limited when it comes to dealing with moral questions. For the professionalizing of any area
of knowledge tends to produce "minds in a groove," to use
Alfred North Whitehead's phrase, grooves which, he adds,
result in a "restraint of serious thought." The result is that the
"remainder of life tends to be treated superficially, with the
imperfect categories of thought derived from one profession."[21]
We shall say more about this limitation in chapter four. Professional ethics thus tends inevitably to become a professionalization of ethics. The critical element becomes accountability to one's peers. Professionals insist that they must assess
themselves, on the rationale that no one outside the profession has sufficient knowledge, experience, or authority to do
so. But what is the range of accountability embraced by such
moral sensitivity? The powerful forces of professionalization
clearly engender a deep sense of what is appropriate and what
is not, but professionals are not prone to have as part of their
animating spirit an outlet to a broader sphere. Indeed, the practice of law claims so much of a person's time, energy, and resources, that it is not surprising that the moral ethos of lawyers
should be quite strong in resisting what is perceived as alien
influence.[22]

Yet for lawyers to seek expert help at times from ethicists
would not be an acknowledgment of intellectual or moral in-
adequacy, but simply an eminently sensible way to secure a
new perspective on their professional lives. For the moral phil-
osopher does not claim to have a better vision of what it is to
be a good human person than does the attorney, but rather
a different vision, a complementary dimension, namely that
of ultimacy. Such a dimension encourages attorneys to rethink
particular moral dilemmas in the context of their freedom to
decide upon the goals of legality as well as the goals of advocacy. This different but not better perspective presses the
lawyer to a renewed critical examination of social structures.
What kind of society are we creating by one or other choice
in the legal field? To whom ought one be responsible? Lawyers
cannot deal with such questions without distancing themselves

from day to day preoccupations, and dialogue with ethicists would force them to do just this. But such dialogue will help the ethicists as well, by giving them concrete matters of real importance upon which to focus their theories. The current crisis of ethical perplexity in the legal profession ought therefore to be seen as an opportunity and a challenge. To call upon people outside this profession in the area of morals is to strengthen both law and morals, just as dialogue between law and economics, medicine, and pyschology strengthens all these professions in turn.[23]

I have one corollary to add to these remarks regarding the incompleteness of both law and lawyers. Earlier I suggested that the conflict encouraged by our adversary system does not necessarily promote justice for those segments of society that are rarely involved in litigation. Lawyers in general would not accept this. For "thinking like a lawyer" means believing that this adversary system and all its legal tools are ideally suited for solving problems of justice. Even such a penetrating critic as Monroe Freedman, who has been widely and justly praised for his candid scrutiny of the Code of Professional Responsibility, assumes at the outset of his study that any free society, predicated on respect for human dignity, will depend upon the unimpeded operation of the adversarial process.[24] When lawyers are faced with an area of life outside the legal system where things are not going as they should, their solution is inevitably to expand the legal system in order to bring that area within it.

Yet the interests of poor and less sophisticated litigants, who have few resources to press their cases, would seem to dictate just the opposite solution, namely to contract the legal system, thereby removing from the adversarial area such matters as divorce and probate, or the loss of a franchise, or the theft of a patent, or the default of a pension scheme. These need not be adversarial in character at all, as we have found in the case of no-fault automobile insurance. In other words, justice in society ought not necessarily be linked at all with lawyers and law suits. In order to think about justice a person need not have to think of himself or herself as a litigant.[25] Nor can the maldistributive aspects of adversary justice really be mitigated all that much by expanding the public interest bar or government legal services. As valuable as these recent expansions have been in American life, they are bound to be spotty and incomplete.

Rather what is needed is a recognition that justice is a much wider concept than legality, and that resources for its promotion need not depend exclusively upon law or lawyers. For both are inherently limited when it comes to setting the parameters of morality in public life.

Let me draw one conclusion from these remarks on public morality. The laws of any country are indeed the mode by which a people creates its civilization and culture. But of themselves these laws can achieve justice only approximately. And even this approximation of justice must often be worked out in ambiguous circumstances. Unfortunately Americans have very low tolerance for such ambiguity. We stubbornly refuse to admit that the best we can do is to approximate justice in most of our institutions. On the contrary, we tend to believe that, because laws aim to delineate what is just and unjust, their literal observance guarantees the moral and the good. Whereas in fact almost every law has to be interpreted, by judges most of all, but also by lawyers, police, and all who make decisions in the public realm. Sometimes these individuals may operate in clarity and light, but much more often their arena is that shadowy no man's land of human discretion, where pursuit of what is lawful and wise is continually challenged by new understandings of the common good.

Public morality depends upon the freedom which produces such approximations of justice, even though law itself seeks to escape from the resulting ambiguity. This is why governments, like human beings themselves, must be judged ultimately as products not of law but of freedom. For, unlike law, the staple of human freedom is seldom that of logic and reason. John Henry Newman noted this over a century ago and his words have a special application today to the phenomenon of morality in public life: "Quarry the granite rock with razors, or moor the vessel with a thread of silk; then may you hope with such keen and delicate instruments as human knowledge and human reason to contend against those giants, the passion and pride of man."[26]

4

Law as Vocation

The legal profession in the United States is at present a beleaguered institution. Conservatives criticize it for reaching too far into the economic and social spheres; liberals criticize it for being unavailable to those who cannot afford its cost; radicals criticize it for becoming an instrument of oppression and exploitation. There are many who think American society is law-drenched: we have altogether too much law and too many lawyers. Facts support this judgment. As I mentioned in the last chapter, there are now over 600,000 lawyers in the nation, one for every 388 people; two-thirds of all the lawyers in the world live here; and one third of these, almost 200,000, have been in practice less than five years. The number of civil suits filed in federal courts has more than doubled since 1960 and increased by more than a third since 1970. The clog in state courts is even worse: in Cook County in Chicago, to choose one example, a negligence case can take as long as four years to get to trial. This rise in civil litigation comes at a time when courts are already inundated with criminal cases. Violent crime has increased by almost 200 percent since 1960, and the total number of crimes by over 180 percent.[1]

What is going on in American society and in the legal profession? There seems to be general agreement that the unique role of the lawyer as an independent advocate is being eroded by a rapidly growing segment of the American bar that views law as a business rather than as a profession. The large multistate law firms are growing ever larger, and their complexity and bureaucracy inevitably chill their members' professional independence as well as isolate them from the humanity of their clients. A Harris poll several years ago, rating public confidence in 16 institutions, found law firms at the bottom, along with Congress, organized labor, and advertising agencies. Somehow there is a sense that in the public sphere the profession as a whole is not functioning for the common good and that public virtue is not its main concern. But why? Historically the very concept of "profession" connoted not private self-interest but service to society, though we must remember that this concept was born at a time when the legal profession was still secured to a generally accepted moral and religious foundation.

In the pages that follow I would like to begin with our western concept of profession, as this was originally formulated, along with its companion concept of "calling." On this level our question becomes not so much "What kind of a lawyer does a person want to be?" but "What kind of a person does a lawyer want to be?" It will also be clear that, while a lawyer's "vocation" is clearly to promote justice in society, it ought also to be conceived as a vocation to love. Our difficulties begin as soon as we move from this abstract level to the concrete functioning of the profession in America. For then we immediately recognize how much this profession has been conditioned over the years by the traditionally litigious character of American society as well as by what American jurists have generally conceived to be the nature of American law. If we go on to examine the present state of the legal profession and the type of education given to the typical American law student, we find even more problems. None of these can be either ignored or minimized if we want a realistic understanding of how someone can function as a lawyer in America today and still be true to his or her commitment of service to society. For such a person will have to deal not only with conflicts of justice between persons but also with conflicts of the spirit that are far more threatening and painful.

I

We can speak of someone being "called" to a profession because of the way we have traditionally understood "profession" in the West. The term "profession" became secularized in the English language about the mid-seventeenth century, following its more restricted earlier usage to signify the taking of vows in a religious order. The concept itself, however, goes back to Graeco-Roman thought, especially as applied to the technical skills of lawyers and physicians. The Middle Ages added to the concept the requirement of university education in the arts and sciences, in order to support specialty skills with rational theory and a broad cultural background. Eventually the concept developed a third feature, in addition to skills and learning, namely those autonomous associations of professionals that defined their members' standards of performance and provided sanctions for any violation. Hence certain characteristics have come to be associated with all professional activity: a high degree of generalized and systematic knowledge, as well as technical competence in a specialized area; an orientation that is primarily to community service rather than to individual self-interest; significant behavior control through internalized codes of ethics, formulated by voluntary organizations run by the professionals themselves.

Professions are distinguished from other occupations in that they justify their activities in terms other than self-interest. Because the superior knowledge associated with them gives power and control in a community, it is important that such knowledge be used primarily in the community interest. Consequently the reward system in professions consists not just in money, but in prestige, awards, and community status. Professionals are also rewarded with a client's trust, and indeed ask for such trust, because they profess to know better than their clients what ails them and their affairs. While they claim the right to treat their clients by virtue of their specialized learning, they also pledge not to exploit this situation for personal gain:

> These characteristics and collective claims of a profession are dependent upon a close solidarity, upon its members constituting in some measure a group apart with an ethos of its own. This in turn implies deep and lifelong commitment. A man who leaves a profession, once he is fully trained, licensed, and initiated, is something of a renegade in the eyes of his fellows. . . . It takes a rite of passage to get him in; another to read him out. If he takes French leave, he seems to belittle the profession and his former colleagues.[2]

From what we have said so far, it is not difficult to see why the concept of vocation has been linked so closely to that of profession: the sense of commitment is central to both, even after the concept of vocation has been totally secularized. The legal profession has even been compared to a secular national religion in America. "I often feel that I am a black-robed priest," writes one judge.[3] The respect accorded to law in our national life does in fact give to law some of the qualities of a religion, and to the legal profession a resemblance to priesthood. Legal ritual, like religious ritual, provides coherence and form within a disorderly society. Lawyers are seen as secular clergy, praying before the court, while judges are seen as secular bishops who wear flowing robes and sit on raised platforms above all others in the courtroom. "A trial with its controlled forms of address, cross-examination, and procedural orderliness, offers a comforting framework to dispel feelings of helplessness. . . . The bar, like the church, relies upon mysterious language and procedures to instill reverence. . . . The black robes of bishop and judge clothe mere mortals with the power of the Lord or the law. The courtroom is our cathedral, where contemporary passion plays are enacted. In both buildings silence, awe, and deference—if not subservience—placate the authorities."[4]

But the concept of vocation as applied to the legal profession has other and more important connotations than that of civil religion. Just as the major concern of medicine has always been for health, so that of law has always been for justice. Law as a vocation is thus primarily to be understood as a striving for justice. Indeed, law has often been referred to as the art of doing justice. Trying to define justice as the goal of law, however, is as difficult as trying to define "health" as the goal of medicine. Like "beauty" these professional ideals elude rational analysis. It is much easier to recognize their opposites, injustice and sickness. For the lawyer and physician this is also more important. The problem for the legal profession, nevertheless, is the perennial temptation to equate justice with the administration of justice, thereby assuming that government in the person of the judge is the source of justice. Just legal procedures are obviously of paramount importance in a pluralistic society, but exclusive reliance upon them can result in thinking and speaking of justice in terms of coercion rather than truth.[5] This is why in the 1972 Oliver Wendell Holmes, Jr., Lectures at Harvard, John Noonan of Berkeley could say that the "central problem . . . of the legal enterprise is the relation of love to power. We can often apply force to those we do not see, but we cannot, I think, love them. Only in the response of person to person can Augustine's sublime fusion be achieved, in which justice is defined as 'love serving only the one loved.' "[6] It is thus a mistake to build a chasm between justice and love as these have relevance to the legal profession.

The classic understanding of justice, originating in natural law theory, was that of giving to each person his or her due. Justice in this sense was thought to be the foundation of civil society. What Augustine asserted, however, was that civil society is in reality *not* always based upon the principle of giving every person his or her due, but is rather based upon and held together by what persons love (which for Augustine could be a bad love or a good love). In Book XIX of *The City of God* Augustine distinguishes between societies informed by the love of power and those informed by the power of a good love, and he then analyzes at length how love functions as the bond of civil society. In this analysis justice becomes the form of love and the standard of love, which expresses the right ordering of human relations with reference to God's order and purpose. Love is thus the key perspective for fashioning as well as criticizing law. Without a just love there can be no right order in society, since the public sphere would otherwise not only be continually disturbed by human willfulness, but persons would also lack any real motive to render to others their due.

According to Augustine, then, justice to persons may be identified with a right love, and it is then expressed as an active service to another who is loved. This understanding of justice is so important because, as we shall see later in more detail, lawyers are conditioned by their training and practice to think in terms of rules and problems rather than persons. An exclusive concern for justice, understood professionally in its more procedural and administrative sense, is therefore clearly inadequate as a vocational ideal for the lawyer, educator, or judge. Even understood in its larger sense as the principle that every person is entitled to his or her due, justice as a virtue must be complemented by the virtues of compassion and hope so necessary in the interpersonal lives of lawyers and clients. "The process is rightly understood only if rules and persons are seen as equally essential components, every rule depending on persons to frame, apply, and undergo it, every person using rules. Rules and persons in the analysis of law are complementary. By the same token, the paradigm of the impartial judge and the paradigm of the personally responsible judge are equally necessary."[7]

To contrast law and love, the one abstract, objective, and impersonal, the other concrete, subjective, and personal, is to misunderstand the nature of law, according to Harvard Professor Harold J. Berman. Law does not consist of general rules but is rather a process, a living social institution for *applying* general rules. As such it is concrete, subjective, and personal. To think of it otherwise would be to treat justice as a purely intellectual problem. "There is nothing abstract or impersonal," says Berman, "about putting a man in jail because he committed a robbery, or enjoining the School Board of Little Rock, Arkansas, from excluding Negroes from the Central High School, or awarding a man who has been run down by an automobile money damages to pay his hospital bills. Law is not only rules and concepts; law is also, and primarily, a type of relationship among people. . . . The contrast between law and love exaggerates the role of rules in law and underestimates the role of decision and of relationship; further, it exaggerates the role of spontaneity in love, and underestimates the role of deliberation and restraint."[8]

To speak of law as a vocation to justice and love is thus to unite what tends to be separated in the professional life of the lawyer. Justice functions also on the interpersonal level, and love functions also on the social level. Thomas Shaffer sounds the leitmotiv of what we shall be discussing shortly, when he says that the legal culture of justice in America finds it very hard to say that a lawyer's life is really a ministry and that this ministry aims beyond justice to compassion and hope. "Compassion is the heart of counseling and counseling is what lawyers do most of the time. Lawyers do not, most of the time 'dispense' or 'administer' or serve justice: they serve people who know and who want to know how to live together. The professional culture's proclaimed concern with justice, because justice is often irrelevant to this enterprise, makes compassion more rather than less difficult."[9]

Just how difficult will be apparent shortly. For what we have been doing thus far is speaking in theory. We must now examine very concretely the four major aspects of America's legal culture which condition a lawyer's vocation to justice and love, and in large measure tend to inhibit its realization. I refer to the nature of American society, the nature of American law, the nature of American legal education, and the nature of the

American legal profession. Only after such an examination can we talk realistically of how an individual attorney, in the light of this conditioning, can still consider his or her life as a vocation to justice and love.

II

The legal profession in the United States developed gradually over two centuries in accordance with certain characteristics that were and continue to be endemic to American society. Alexis de Tocqueville observed as early as 1835 that "there is hardly a political question in the United States that does not sooner or later turn into a judicial one."[10] The source of this impetus was the pervasive influence of the British common law tradition, imported very early into the colonies to dominate the colonial legal system. As it originated, the common law of England (i.e., law formulated by judges as opposed to statutory law enacted by legislative bodies) was law developed by and for aristocrats. Legal historian Lawrence Friedman underlines this: "Leaf through the pages of Lord Coke's reports, compiled in the late 16th and early 17th century; here one will find a colorful set of litigants, all drawn from the very top of British society—lords and ladies, landed gentry, high-ranking clergymen, wealthy merchants. . . . The masses were hardly touched by this system and only indirectly under its rule."[11]

All this changed when the Colonies gained independence. These "rights by Englishmen," elaborated over centuries in great detail by the English judiciary, now became democratized. The new nation was in fact founded on law and on a legal system that was centered on litigation. Historian Maxwell Bloomfield notes that in postrevolutionary times "a middle class public, cherishing the ideals of competition, utilitarianism, and self-advancement, found itself unwilling to forego the advantages of an individualistic legal system in favor of some more equitable communitarian equipment."[12] The Bill of Rights referred to the rights of everyone. Democracy brought with it the idea that the people themselves could direct their own affairs and that they could use law to accomplish this. Americans took literally the language of their Constitution, their charters and statutes. "What good is a right that cannot, be enforced and pleaded in court? If a right is observed there is no need to turn to judges; but if it is disregarded, to whom else ought one turn?"[13]

This dominant ethic of competitive individualism, that has been part of the American psyche from the beginning, inevitably fostered an adversary culture. The United States was, after all, founded by persons preoccupied with the assertion and maintenance of individual rights. Government, according to the Founders, was to be checked, with power balanced against power, so that personal liberty would remain intact. The great immigrations of the nineteenth and twentieth centuries brought millions who were distrustful of the government they knew in Europe and zealous to embrace and maintain their rights in the new world. Our classical liberal tradition is thus based on a fragmented model of society that emphasizes a negative responsibility to restrain power and to resist any clear center to the social system. No one will deny that the American emphasis upon personal freedom and competition has mobilized powerful energies in the nation, but it has also encouraged an open litigiousness based on rights claimed, adjudicated, and enforced. Such litigiousness is not a legal but a social phenomenon. It exists in other nations, of course, but in much more muted form, and in some eastern cultures, like that of Japan for example, it is almost totally unknown.

This native adversary culture has been exacerbated during the past two generations by another American phenomenon: the radical separation of legal and religious values. Such separation has resulted from the triumph of the Enlightenment concept of law as something wholly instrumental and wholly invented, a pragmatic device for accomplishing specific political, economic, and social objectives. We shall say more about this in the next section. For now it is important to realize that this totally secular understanding of law, which goes back to the French and American revolutions and has for over a century been espoused by most American jurists, has only recently penetrated the general social consciousness. Its parallel concept is that of religion as a wholly private affair, without any political or social dimension, and with no role to play in overcoming the forces of public disorder and strife. Harold Berman has emphasized that this secularizing of law and this spiritualizing of religion is something quite different from the separation of church and state mandated by the Constitution, i.e., the separation of religious from political and legal *institutions*. The contemporary phenomenon under scrutiny here is rather the almost total absence of any interaction between religious and legal *values*.[14]

I said a moment ago that our adversary culture was aggravated by this phenomenon. The reason is that without such interaction law tends to degenerate into legalism and to rely exclusively on coercive sanction to secure obedience rather than upon experiences of fairness and trust. "It is precisely when law is trusted," says Berman, "and therefore does not require coercion . . . that it is efficient. One who rules by law is not compelled to be present anywhere with his police force. . . . In the last analysis, what deters crime is the tradition of being law-abiding, and this in turn depends upon a deeply or passionately held conviction that law is not only an instrument of secular policy, but also part of the ultimate purpose and ultimate meaning of life."[15] Banning from the realm of law the religious and moral discourse common to most Americans is thus to hasten the decay of that civility between persons which finally enables the legal system to service its fundamental goals of justice, mercy, and community trust.

What we have operating in contemporary American society, then, is an instinctive national impulse to rely upon litigation to settle disputes, coupled with the relatively recent isolation of that impulse from those religious values which counsel prudence, civility, reflection, and trust. The consequent breakdown in community has fed the current explosion of lawsuits, which in turn has accelerated the breakdown of community. Several other sociological factors compound the problem. A change in our economic base is perhaps the most significant. American society is gradually being transformed from an industrial to an information-based society, in which people interact far more than ever before with other people. "The number of personal and business transactions has increased geometrically, encompassing a broad range of activities on paper and over wires, including phone calls, letters, messages, bills, checks, contracts, and agreements. Because the medium we trade in is information—words, ideas, communications—we have become a more litigious society as some transactions undoubtedly go sour or are thrown into question."[16] A rising population is another factor. When people are concentrated in a single area, the greater the number of collisions they tend to have with each other. There are also more young people and more old people in the United States today, and these usually have far more problems than the middle-aged. Finally, there is the ever increasing willingness in the nation to let courts settle matters that were once settled by legislatures, executives, parents, teachers, or just pure chance. Judges are now asked to run prisons, hospitals, and school systems and their decisions may even in some cases replace those of physicians, labor unions, and parents.

This last factor, however, the growing reliance upon courts, is not totally negative. On the one hand the result has been an almost hopeless congestion in court dockets. The six Federal District Courts in New York, New Jersey, and Connecticut, for example, between 1978 and 1983 had an increase of new cases that ranged between 44 and 140, a range of increase that reflects the situation in most of the other 94 District Courts across the country.[17] But from another point of view such massive litigation, especially in federal courts, can be judged an index of societal health. The reason is that, following the *Brown* decision in 1954, the Supreme Court demonstrated an unprecedented sensitivity to the legal rights of disadvantaged citizens. "As courts impeded discrimination based on race, gender, or wealth, a generation of Americans looked to a vigorous, vigilant judiciary to enforce the Bill of Rights. The judiciary developed procedural safeguards in criminal law, protected the rights of the indigent, and expanded the right to counsel. New rules—superseding old notions of who could sue or be sued, and about what—reduced the immunity of public officials and enlarged litigation opportunities for victims of discrimination, harassment, and official lawlessness."[18]

Besides the judicial activism in the 1950s and 1960s Americans pursued the goal of equality in other ways. Public interest law firms developed along with a Federal Legal Services program. The underprivileged and disadvantaged could now file class-action lawsuits and use litigation to expose closed institutions like prisons and hospitals to public scrutiny and government regulation. Over the last generation the American impulse to litigate has thus to some extent at least been transformed into the vital ingredients of social justice. This is why we cannot evaluate our litigiousness outside the context of true injuries to people and their right of redress. Plaintiffs sue to heal these injuries and to vindicate these rights, and so the judiciary has inevitably become the ultimate authority that defines legally redressable injury.

III

Despite this positive side of increased reliance upon courts, the litigious character of American society that we have just discussed remains overall one of the problematic factors in any person's pursuit of law as a vocation to justice and love. A second factor is the nature of American law itself. Practicing lawyers seldom think about the nature of law, and their penalty for avoiding such reflection is to be without any sense of the presuppositions underlying their profession and shaping their everyday lives as attorneys. But merely because most lawyers are unconcerned with a legal worldview does not mean that they do not have one or that it is not operative in their lives. As Douglas Sturm has said, jurisprudence is unavoidable for a lawyer. "One may not think about breathing but one breathes anyway. One may not deliberate about the economic system of a country, but one nonetheless fulfills some role in it. One's jurisprudence, however unsophisticated or subliminal, is nevertheless played out in one's conduct at law."[19]

Is there a particular jurisprudence actually functioning in America today? There seems to be no question that what has come to be called legal realism is the living worldview of the average American lawyer. If presented with the issue, he or she would surely say that such realism is the most attractive theory of law for someone who wants to win a close case, or to counsel a businessman about to enter a complex commercial transaction. Legal realism sees law as simply a means to implement whatever social values and behavior are desired by a society at any given time. Realists therefore reject the idea of permanent rules or principles that have authority to determine what ought to be the outcome of a given case. Rather, they say, the outcome of a case depends largely, if not entirely, on the predilections of the judge who happens to be deciding it. These decisions, in turn, can be thought of as "rules," but only in a purely instrumental sense: they may be useful in telling us what we may expect in future court decisions. Thus, for Karl Llewellyn, realism is "distrust of traditional legal rules and concepts insofar as they purport to *describe* what either courts or people are actually doing." And Jerome Frank tells us that "the way in which the judge gets his hunches is the key to the judicial process."[20] This process is thus inseparably linked to politics, economics, and culture.

The origins of legal realism go back to the legal positivism of the last century. Realists and positivists both see the nature of law to be law as it is and not law as it ought to be. Positivists, however, usually abstract from the values of what is going on in a given society, whereas realists, while acknowledging and even stressing the relationship between law and social values, scrupulously abstain from any critical judgment on these values. Oliver Wendell Holmes, Jr., one of the architects of legal positivism in America, could thus define law as "prophesies of what the courts will do in fact, and nothing more pretentious."[21] Law thus represents what a society is like at any particular time; it reflects the values of a greater culture.

In 1881 Holmes opened his study of *The Common Law* with this statement: "The life of the law has not been logic: it has been experience. The felt necessities of the time, the prevalent moral and political theories, intentions of public policy, avowed or unconscious, even the prejudices which judges share with their fellowmen, have had a good deal more to do than the syllogism in determining the rules by which men would be governed."[22] To know what law is, said Holmes, one must look upon it as a "bad man" does. The "bad man" has no respect for law as such and does not look upon it as telling him what is right or wrong. He obeys only if it is in his interest to obey. The threat of coercive sanction is what keeps him from disobedience. He thinks of law "as simply part of the environment in which he does his business. He may break a contract, pay the assessed damages, and think little of it, so long as, on balance, his self-defined welfare has been served. . . . Law is a neutral object to be used where it might benefit, to be avoided where it might hurt, and to be put into the balance of calculations as one sets out one's policies for the future."[23]

Although Holmes was the first American to articulate in any complete way a positivist legal theory, the groundwork for such theory was laid by the rigid positivism of Thomas Hobbes. It was Hobbes who forced the decisive breach between theology and jurisprudence. The only human motive worth taking seriously, said Hobbes in *Leviathan*, is self preservation. Humans have only desires and appetites, and a good society can be created only by well articulated self-interest. Hobbes considered human beings so irretrievably selfish and predatory that they had to be restrained by the absolute authority of the state. His understanding of lawlessness is the decisive element in his account of the source of law, for by lawlessness he means not only the absence of positive law but the absence of any awareness among humans of what is right and wrong. In this conflict model of society, law becomes essentially a matter of force and coercion and not of substantive justice, an instrument to be used to secure order and to enhance one's struggle for power. Holmes was echoing Hobbes when he wrote that "the *ultima ratio*, not only [of kings], but of private persons, is force, and . . . at the bottom of all private relations, however tempered by sympathy and all the social feelings, is a justifiable self-preference." For Holmes, as for Hobbes, the function of law was simply to channel these private aggressions in an orderly fashion. Like Hobbes, he also believed that law had nothing at all to do with morality, and could, if the majority of citizens so decided, promote what was immoral. "The first requirement of a sound body of law is, that it should correspond with the actual feelings and demands of the community, whether right or wrong."[24]

While contemporary legal realists would not judge humans as harshly as Hobbes, or even Holmes for that matter, most would nevertheless espouse a conflict model of society. Learned Hand's definition of justice, for example, was "the tolerable accommodation of the conflicting interests of society." Justice is thus seen as a compromise, giving the least offense to the most people, some rough equation between order and fairness. Even a humanist like Karl Llewellyn can write that in law we see

> the phenomenon of clashing interests of antagonistic persons or groups, with officials stepping in to favor some as against others. . . . Hence the eternal fight for the machinery of law, and of law-making, whereby the highly interested *A*s can hope partially to force their will upon equally but adversely interested *B*s and to put behind that control the passive approval and support of the great body of *C*s.[25]

For Llewellyn, as for legal realists and positivists generally, it is important to isolate the uniqueness of law, to underline its autonomy and to differentiate it from other forms of thought and action. Pushed to extremes, this makes law purely instrumental, a pragmatic device for accomplishing primarily individualistic political or economic objectives in society. Such extremes are in fact integral to the thought of legal theorists like Hans Kelsen, who argues that "the concept of law has no moral connotations whatsoever." To say that a certain social order has the character of law, insists Kelsen, "does not imply the moral judgment that this order is good or just. There are legal orders which are, from a certain point of view, unjust. Law and justice are two different concepts."[26] Few realists and positivists would go as far as Kelsen. Nor would they go as far as Holmes, who once wrote in a letter to a friend: "I have said to my brethren [on the Supreme Court] many times that I hate justice, which means that I know if a man begins to talk about that, for one reason or another he is shirking thinking in legal terms."[27] Most of today's jurists would say that, while an analysis of the *is* of factual legal situations should not get entangled with any *ought to be*, the professional decisions of individual lawyers are never merely technical. At every level these decisions are controlled by value judgments of what ought or ought not to be. But a realist like Llewellyn would insist that with such value judgments "we desert entirely the solid sphere of objective observations, of possible agreement among all trained observers, and enter the airy sphere of individual ideals and subjectivity."[28] In other words, even if values are involved, they remain highly individualistic preferences, without any logical entailments intrinsic to law itself.

For the positivists and the realists, then, the true essence of law is how disputes are settled by judges and administrators. The rules of law are simply generalized statements of the behavior pattern of officials, the source of which is to be found chiefly outside the law, in the policies, prejudices and preferences of these officials. "What . . . *officials do about disputes is, to my mind, the law itself,*" says Llewellyn.[29] This generally agreed-upon understanding of law in America has inevitably fostered an adversary ethic, which, when combined with the litigious character of American society discussed earlier, produces the "fight" theory of justice. Out of this theory has come our adversary system. It assumes that in the competitive strife of a courtroom, the lawyers defending each litigant will energetically use all the available evidence favorable to their client and unfavorable to their adversary. The trial court will thereby obtain all the relevant evidence and will consequently be able to apply to the actual facts the social policies embodied in the legal rules. In theory at least, such an adversary system supposedly gives to each person the means to defend his or her rights and interests. This in turn vindicates the American concept of the good society as one that secures the life, liberty, and property of its individual citizens, and gives to each an equitable share of society's goods, roughly approximating our notions of distributive justice. For the legal realist the benefits to society are therefore clear:

> Litigation arises out of conflict. Conflict in turn arises in those fields of social activity where growth is taking place, where the relative strength of interest-groups is changing. Things are so arranged that where changing social practice demands new law individual interest will see to it that suits will be brought which will furnish a substratum for the elaboration of the legal doctrine. There is happily a kind of automatic correlation between the interest of the individual litigant and the social need for new law.[30]

The justification of the adversary system is not difficult in the case of criminal prosecution. There its purpose is both to protect the innocent person against the possibility of an unjust conviction, as well as to preserve the integrity of society itself. It aims at keeping sound the procedures by which society goes about condemning and punishing the criminal, and as such it has great symbolic value. In criminal law, therefore, the case for zealous advocacy is easy to make. American society especially, with its strong commitment to political freedom, has always valued any means that deters government from imprisoning those it distrusts and fears. The adversary system, by putting the heavy burden of proof on the state and at the same time guaranteeing to defendants access to loyal and independent advocates, prevents oppression by the state.

The real problems in the system begin to appear when it is taken out of the context of criminal prosecution and placed within a larger community context. Then public interest tends to be conceived almost exclusively in terms of the rights and interests of individual clients. While there may be obvious adversary behavior on the part of someone who breaks a contract, making enforced compliance by trial quite proper, most forms of human activity are not adversarial at all. "The parents'

role is not normally to oppose the child. The doctor's intent
is to help, not to injure. But the growing desire for redress of
injuries prompts us more and more to search for the wrong-
doer. That search leads us with increasing frequency to view
conduct and relationships as conflicting that not so long ago
were unhesitatingly accepted as altruistic or benign."[31]

John Wigmore, who wrote the classic legal textbook on evidence, called the adversary system "the greatest legal engine
ever invented for the discovery of truth."[32] But the most common ground for criticizing the system today is precisely its in-
capacity to uncover the truth.[33] Mutual exaggeration of opposing claims, so widely accepted in practice, violates the whole
theory of rational, scientific investigation. As a means of un-
covering facts, the system can be extremely slow and inefficient, and its endless formalities and opportunities to delay
make it terribly expensive. This means that generally the system will work for the naturally litigious and for the wealthy,
but not for the poor. Public defenders and members of the
public interest bar, who defend those unable to pay litigation
costs, are usually overworked and ill equipped, and the services they give are bound to be spotty in application and dis-
tribution. If their battle is against more intelligent fighters who
are better paid, more experienced or more vicious, they will
usually lose. The Legal Services Corporation, moreover, estimates that it can service only a fraction of the poor people who
need legal help. The interests of poorer and less sophisticated
litigants would be much better served by removing their claims
from the adversarial arena altogether. For in that area they will
find themselves more or less helpless and threatened, with
their rights unprotected, their liberty threatened, and their
property unsecured. Because it depends on force, the adversary system is thus inevitably biased toward the strong and
seldom serves the aspirations of the general community. But
then American culture as a whole, as we have seen, is not particularly communitarian, and its legal system will, in all likelihood, continue to follow suit with an emphasis on pragmatism,
conflict, and coercion.

IV

The third factor inhibiting someone's pursuit of law as a
vocation to justice and love is the nature of American legal

education. The character and content of such education would seem to follow logically from both the nature of American law and the nature of American society. And so it does, as we shall see presently. But American legal education also has a peculiar history of its own, conditioned by something quite distinct from (and in ironic tension with) either realism as a legal theory or the litigiousness of Americans generally. This "something" is the drive for classifications and systemization, a phenomenon that began in 1871, when Christopher Langdell of Harvard, Dean of one of the very few law schools in the country at the time, formally announced his creation of the case method for the study of law.

The problem Langdell faced as a teacher was that in late nineteenth century America there already was too much law (i.e. too many cases in too many courts in too many state and federal institutions) to serve as a basis for organized study at a university (as opposed to the more usual way of then becoming a lawyer by apprenticing oneself to a practicing attorney). To deal with law as an organized body of knowledge, i.e. as a university discipline, one had to find a way to make sense out of all these cases. There had to be an identifiable body of information about law that would serve as the proper subject matter for study, and there also had to be a method of inquiry that would train a student to "think like a lawyer." Langdell's solution was an ingenious combination of the abstract and the concrete. "Law, considered as a science," he wrote, "consists of certain principles or doctrines. To have such a mastery of these as to be able to apply them with constant facility and certainty to the ever-tangled skein of human affairs, is what constitutes the true lawyer; and hence to acquire that mastery should be the business of every earnest student of law. Each of these doctrines has arrived at its present state by slow degrees; in other words it is a growth, extending in many cases through centuries. This growth is to be traced in the main through a series of cases; and much of the shortest and best, if not the only way of mastering doctrine effectually is by studying the cases in which it is embodied".[34]

Langdell's original idea, then, was that law is a science and that legal truth is a species of scientific truth: once the one true rule of law in a given area has been discovered, it will continue without change, reducing the unruly diversity of cases to manageable unity. In his brilliant study, *The Ages of American Law*, Grant Gilmore points out that before Langdell legal texts contained the bare minimum of theoretical discussion; what counted was what real people were doing in the real world. What counted with Langdell, however, was precisely the theory, the unitary set of rules that made sense of the cases which illustrate the rules. Hence not all cases were to be studied. The vast majority of these, said Langdell, are worse than useless for any purpose of systematic study. In other words, the rule of law does not in any sense emerge from the study of real cases decided in the real world. "The doctrine tests the cases, not the other way around."[35] With this we are at strange odds with the dominant strand of contemporary legal theory represented by realism.

In 1881, in *The Common Law*, Oliver Wendell Holmes, Jr., gave Langdell's pedagogical approach a certain intellectual respectability. Holmes developed a philosophical hypothesis that all progress in law and legal rules is toward an ideal state in which liability, both civil and criminal, will be governed by objective standards, not by a person's subjective state of mind or intent to cause harm. As a legal system approached maturity, said Holmes, it will succeed in eliminating any reference to what the defendant actually thought or willed. Individual guilt or moral failure would both become irrelevant, and law would deal with the "bad man" and the "good man" in exactly the same way.[36] This was in fact the ideal behind Langdell's approach to the law of contracts and the law of torts. Before Langdell legal education dealt with as many types of contracts as there were classes of people who entered into them: contracts among farmers, workers, merchants, brokers, auctioneers, seamen, corporations, shipowners, and between landlords and tenants, husbands and wives, parents and children – all these were studied by law students precisely as different, conditioned by circumstances, people, and content. Langdell, however, insisted that neither the status of the contracting parties nor the subject matter of their contract was to be taken into account in the "science of law." Law study should focus not upon people, but only upon "faceless characters named A & B, whoever they might be and whatever it might be they were trying to accomplish." The study of "torts,"i.e. personal injuries or noncontractual losses, was to be approached in the same way. "As with the new theory of contracts, the new theory of torts was designed to cover all possible situations in which any A might be ordered to pay damages to any B to compensate him for personal injury or property damage, with as little account as possible taken of who A and B were and the particular circumstances of their confrontation."[37]

Langdell and Holmes together set a tone and a style for legal education that have lasted over a century. The American law school became over the years the principal instrument for restructuring our jurisprudence and reshaping our legal system. What future lawyers studied now were unitary theories to explain all conceivable single instances, and it was no longer necessary for them to take into account what was going on in the real world. For law had become a "science," whose laboratory, as Langdell said, was the law library and whose experimental materials were the printed case books. Rules were separated from flesh and blood people and law itself ceased to be considered a human activity affecting those acting and those acted upon, and became rather a set of technical skills to be mastered and applied first in the classroom and later in law office and courts. Rules became the subject matter of legal study and the function of the "case" was simply to exemplify the rule. Judicial decisions also came in the form of rules, stated in such a way as to be applicable to all similar cases. "Little or no attention is given to the persons in whose minds or in whose interaction the rules have lived—to the persons whose difficulties have occasioned the articulation of the rule, to the lawyers who have tried the case, to the judges who have decided it. . . . The prime teaching tools, the casebooks, have been composed to shed light on the life of the rule, not upon the part of the participants in the process."[38]

Langdell's dream of a system of legal rules that was self-sufficient, absolutely certain, and impervious to change was never fully realized, of course, since American law, as legal realists saw, can never by truly isolated from the economic, political, and social developments in American life. But while the legal realists of modern times might hold up to scorn Langdell's overconceptualization of law, they had no intention whatsoever of abandoning the basic tenets either of Langdell's jurisprudence (that law is a science and that such a thing existed as "the one true rule of law") or of his pedagogy (that the primary task of legal education was that of analysis, classification, and systematization). The realists contented themselves with insisting that Langdell's so-called "rules" of law were simply generalized statements of lawyers' behavior patterns, the source of which was to be found chiefly outside the law, in the policies, prejudices, and preferences of the lawyers themselves. For the realists, "law is a science" was understood to mean "law is a social science."[39]

Now the point I am making by reviewing these developments in American legal education is that they have had, and continue to have today, a decisive effect on how lawyers think about themselves and their craft. "We believe," write the authors of a recent text for law students, "that a subtle process of professionalization occurs during law school without being addressed or even acknowledged. This learning by inadvertence means that the participants often fail to consider fundamental questions about the identity they are assuming, and its relation to their values."[40] This identity has for over a century been shaped by the ability to analyze, the capacity to be precise, logical, and objective. Law students are trained not to make statements which cannot be defended by objective criteria, and so they develop an ability to elaborate legal arguments unconnected with personally-held beliefs. Such legal argument fosters as a result an intellectually narrowing process, with the obvious risk that what is held to be irrelevant to the main argument will gradually in one's thinking become irrelevant altogether. Technical analysis that continually excludes human feeling and concern leads to a sense that these qualities are somehow antithetical to a thoroughly rational inquiry. Justice, however, is something more than the analysis and application of rules, and its achievement requires more than intellectual skills. Indeed, when such skills alone are cultivated, feelings and emotions tend to become dulled, and the lawyer as a human person can lose that sensitivity so essential in a one-to-one relationship with clients. One lawyer has stated the problem in this way:

> Thinking, unabridged by the conscious application of other experience, endorses particular values—the values of order, certainty, and mastery. Such values are not always apposite to, or at least not consistently dominant in, the types of idiosyncratic problems many, if not most, lawyers confront. The unmitigated application of intellect tends to freeze out not only psychological but ethical dispositions as well. . . . The implication for legal education is that, as a general observation, the qualities of personal sensitivity to others, a sense of justice, and concern for the general welfare need to be systematically nur-

tured, rather than developed, else they become overshadowed in the values attendant to concentrated intellectual inquiry.[41]

The risk of over- intellectualization is, of course, a problem common to all professions. As we saw in chapter three, Alfred North Whitehead warned of what he called the "professionalizing" of knowledge. "Each profession makes progress," he wrote,

> but it is progress in its own groove. Now to be mentally in a groove is to live in contemplating a given set of abstractions. The groove prevents straying across country, and the abstraction abstracts from something to which no further attention is paid. . . . Of course, no one is merely a mathematician or merely a lawyer. People have lives outside their professions or their businesses. But the point is the restraint of serious thought within a groove. The remainder of life is treated superficially with the imperfect categories of thought derived from one profession.[42]

It can be the case, then, that the better the professional, the more he or she tends to be preoccupied with correct method and to separate this preoccupation from the interplay of diverse values. This explains why certain kinds of values have almost never been systematically analyzed in law schools: positivists and realists have always considered them unanalyzable, nothing more than inscrutable expressions of personal preference. Law professors may lavish analytic energy in tracing the continuity of values expressed in the opinions of the U. S. Supreme Court, but they generally shy away from any critical scrutiny of these values from the standpoint of either social theory or philosophical ethics. Rarely are students ever encouraged to make judgments regarding the coherence of legal systems with theories of value, much less to supplement the cold logic of legal rules with a responsible and coherent value system of their own. Karl Llewellyn, whom we quoted earlier and who had enormous impact upon legal education, used to tell his first year law students at the University of Chicago that they were welcome to their morals but that these morals had little to do with the culture of lawyers: "The hardest job of the first year is to lop off your common sense, to knock your ethics into temporary anesthesia. Your view of social policy, your sense of justice—to knock these out of you along with woozy thinking, along with ideas all fuzzed along the edges. You are to acquire ability to think precisely, to analyze coldly, . . . to see, and see only, and manipulate, the machinery of the law. It is not easy thus to turn human beings into lawyers. . . . None the less, it is an almost impossible process to achieve the technique without sacrificing some humanity first."[43] But if in principle moral values are irrelevant to legal analysis and professional skill, might one not begin to suppose that living amorally is what it means to be a lawyer, and that being a lawyer is what it means to be a person? Moreover, if no comon judgments of value—either societal or individual value—are possible (but only subjective idiosyncratic preferences), might one not find it very difficult to think of any profession as a vocation to the common good?

Only very recently have any of these problems in American legal education been addressed by the law schools themselves. In its 1984 annual meeting, the Association of American Law Schools for the first time had ethics as its theme. Law school deans and faculty worried especially about the narrowing of ethical perspective, recognizing it as a learned disability, an occupational hazard reinforced later on by the patterns of professional work. "The lack of concern of faculty members for the professional conduct of students," said Norman Redlich, Dean of New York University Law School, "is probably seen by students as a manifestation of similar standards which the faculty members set for themselves." Redlich called on faculty members to explain the importance of professional responsibility as a first step toward "an exploration of a broad range of ethical issues which the profession and the public have a right to expect of us." Speaker after speaker emphasized the heavy responsiblity of faculty to encourage ethical standards by setting examples for their students. Terrance Sandalow, Dean of the University of Michigan Law School, argued that, because law school curricula generally lacked any moral foundation or guiding purpose, individual faculty members had to pay more attention to helping students "to realize their human potential and to act as moral beings." Otherwise, he said, legal education will continue to foster that "curious distinction that lawyers too frequently display—careful craftsmanship in the performance of professional responsibilities and a lack of concern for [craftsmanship] in dealing with political and social issues." Sandalow also called on law schools to place greater emphasis on developing students' "patience, perseverance, and other qualities" that are "necessary to the success of any sustained moral undertaking."[44]

V

The character of American legal education which we have just sketched is directly related to the fourth aspect of our legal culture, the functioning of the legal profession itself. This functioning has come under sharp criticism in recent years, perhaps none sharper than that of Derek Bok, President of Harvard University and former Dean of the Harvard Law School. In his annual report to Harvard's Board of Overseers released in 1983, Bok asserted that the way students were being educated was in large measure responsible for the two major deficiencies of the American legal system, cost and access. "The hallmark of our curriculum," he wrote, "continues to be its emphasis on training students to define the issues carefully and to marshall all the arguments and counterarguments on either side. Law schools celebrate this effort by constantly telling students that they are being taught 'to think like a lawyer.' But one can admire the virtues of careful analysis and still believe that the times cry out for more than these traditional skills. . . . The capacity to think like a lawyer has produced many triumphs, but it has also helped to produce a legal system that is among the most expensive and least efficient in the world." A "flawed system" is Bok's description of the profession as a whole. "There is far too much law for those who can afford it and far too little for those who cannot."[45] What I wish to emphasize here is that these two deficiencies of the system, cost and access, also constitute together a fourth inhibiting factor, originating in the legal profession itself, for anyone pursuing that profession as a vocation to justice and love.

Bok acknowledges, of course, that the root problems with the profession go much deeper than the two deficiencies he focuses upon. Americans generally tend to forget that apprehensions about their legal system correspond to their heavy dependence upon it, stemming from the cultural values and the social structures we opt for as a nation. The difficulties engendered by the litigation explosion of recent years thus cannot be blamed entirely upon lawyers. Lawyers obviously benefit from the fees engendered by American litigiousness, but one can hardly conclude from this that attorneys are the only cause of the nation's propensity to sue. Turning more and more disputes over to the judiciary, as we have done in recent years, clearly contributes to social and economic problems, but the solution does not lie in simply ridiculing the profession. This profession forces lawyers to confront the most vicious as well as the most virtuous aspects of our national life, and to seek continually to bring order out of the chaos of human affairs. People who quote the famous line from Shakespeare's Henry VI, "The first thing we do, let's kill all the lawyers," usually forget that the character who speaks that line, Jack Cade, is contemplating a dictatorship. In a society where government by law is the norm, and where people want the security of law, lawyers are essential. The more laws a nation has, however, the more laws will be broken and the greater use there will be for lawyers and courts. Yet law, as Jerold Auerbach has said, is always more than rules and procedures, statutes and precedents. For Americans it is ultimately a national ideology, a set of beliefs and a system of integrated values that provide elements of predictability, stability, and coherence.[46]

Nevertheless, Bok's question remains: why does the system work so badly for poor people and so well for the affluent? Why does it continually fail its legitimacy test: unable to validate itself to the countless disadvantaged, yet continuing to give special service to the privileged few? "The blunt, inexcusable fact," says Bok, "is that this nation . . . has developed a legal system that is the most expensive in the world, yet cannot manage to protect the rights of most of its citizens." This has happened, he continues, because a certain mindset conditions almost all successful attorneys, all "leaders of the bar." This mindset has two aspects. The first begins in law school, where the educational experience gradually comes to be seen primarily as a conduit to lucrative positions in the big law firms rather than as an opportunity to ponder the larger questions of justice in society. These big firms not only pay well, they also provide the challenge of high-stake litigation and the glamor of social status. For Bok, this overwhelming preference of top graduates for such positions represents "a massive diversion of exceptional talent into pursuits that often add little to the growth of the economy, the pursuit of culture, or the enhancement of the human spirit."[47] The result is a stratification of the bar into an upper and lower tier. The upper tier is drawn from private liberal arts colleges and elite national law schools, and has traditionally consisted of white upperclass males specializing in corporate tax law and antitrust work. In contrast, the lower tier consists mostly of solo practitioners from low status families and less prestigious law schools, who (with some spectacular exceptions in the field of trial practice), tend to rely on the grubbier aspects of practice such as negligence, divorce, and criminal law.

A survey testing the idealism of the 1975 law graduates from the University of California at Davis illustrates what Bok is talking about. Considerable change was shown to have taken place between first and third years. The proportion of those who expected to be working as "poverty" or "public interest" lawyers one year after graduation dwindled from 57 percent in the first year to 22 percent in the third. Those motivated to practice law to "alleviate social problems" fell from 32 percent to 20 percent.[48] "Corporate work seldom interacts with the concerns for social justice that drew me to law school," admitted a 1974 Harvard graduate at his tenth year reunion.[49] Another Harvard student told a friend: "A lot of professors tell me not to worry about politics and just go [to the large firms] for the training; . . . but how do you help U.S. Steel hold up a pollution abatement order during the day, then go home and read your mail from the Sierra Club and tell yourself that you are a human being?"[50] One recent Harvard class had 69 percent entering corporate work, while only 1 percent entered public service. In an address to these graduates Ralph Nader commented on the standards of success held up to them as models by the legal profession:

> Where were we shown images of lawyers as organizers, determined advocates, rather than the disinterested hired hands of whoever could throw the price? . . . Was it really more absorbing to fuss over the details of some company's tax shelter than to face (as our education so seldom asked us to do) the gravest legal problems confronting society—corporate and government corruption, the bilking of consumers, the dilemma of bringing adequate legal services to the poor?[51]

Lloyd N. Cutler, one of Washington's most prominent corporate lawyers, writes the following of large firms like his own: "The rich who pay our fees are less than 1 percent of our fellow citizens, but they get at least 95 percent of our time. The disadvantaged we serve for nothing are perhaps 20 to 25 percent of the population and get at most 5 percent of our time. The remaining 75 percent cannot afford to consult us and get virtually none of our time."[52] This problem is compounded by the fact that there are now so many of these large firms and they are growing ever larger. Ten years ago a dozen or so such firms had over a hundred lawyers; today close to a hundred have this many, and no fewer than sixty have over two hundred. Legal departments of large corporations used to have one or two attorneys; today staffs of fifty or more are not unusual. This slow shift in the profession's legal profile has been primarily responsible for the current efforts of the American Bar Association to revise its Code of Professional Responsibility. The present Code, adopted in 1969, is geared mainly to the solo practitioner, whereas no more than a third of the nation's lawyers now practice by themselves or in small groups. While other factors may influence student choice of a large firm (such as the urgent need to repay loans assumed to finance their legal education), the major reason continues to be the mindset engendered by law schools and the legal culture resulting in what a former president of the Federal Bar Council has called "a dreary metamorphosis of the legal profession to a business."[53] Professional success today, he laments, is measured by profits, and this extreme economic pressure is producing a bottom-line attitude that contributes to rising aggressiveness, incivility, and cutthroat competition, and finally tends to undermine the professional independence of the average American lawyer.

Derek Bok sees a second aspect to this mindset of the professional attorney, one closely linked to the first, namely a willingness to think of justice in purely procedural terms. Such willingness is, of course, a reflection of that legal realism which I discussed earlier. Here is what Bok says:

> At bottom, ours is a society built on individualism, competition, and success. These values bring great personal freedom and mobilize powerful energies. At the same time, they arouse great temptations to shoulder aside one's competitors, to cut corners, to ignore the interests of others in the struggle to succeed. In such a world much responsibility rests upon those who umpire the contest. As society demands higher standards of fairness and decency, the rules of the game tend to multiply and the umpire's burden grows constantly heavier. Faced with these pressures judges and legislators have responded in a man-

ner that reflects our distinctive legal tradition. One hallmark of that tradition is a steadfast faith in intricate procedures where evidence and arguments are presented through an adversary process to a neutral judge who renders a decision on the merits.[54]

The majority of lawyers and judges do in fact think of justice as primarily fair procedure and due process. As essential as these are for the rule of law in any society, however, exclusive focus on them inevitably induces overreliance upon them as well as an overesteem for the adversary system. Bok notes "the familiar tilt of the law curriculum toward preparing students for legal combat." "Look at a typical catalogue," he says. "The bias is evident in the required first-year course in civil procedure, which is typically devoted entirely to the rules of federal courts with no suggestion for other methods of resolving disputes. Looking further, one can discover many courses in the intricacies of trial practice, appellate advocacy, litigation strategy, and the like—but few devoted to methods of mediation and negotiation."[55] Yet the elaborate procedures of the adversary system are precisely the reason that legal services are so expensive and beyond the reach of most ordinary citizens. Those who work in that system look only at the individual case, not at the consequences of rules and decisions in their wider contexts. Laws and jurisdictions multiply into an uncoordinated quilt of rules which, taken together, have unexpected and often untoward social consequences. Because no one is responsible for the system as a whole, no one is able to control either its cost or its access.

The very complexity of these procedures induces in too many lawyers a tunnel-vision, a kind of legal gamesmanship: they raise every argument, no matter how settled the law; they argue points of law they do not themselves believe are right; they file appeals they have no intention of pursuing, simply in order to keep litigation alive; and they continue to dream of the "big case," lavishly financed and staffed, that can drag on in courts for years, until every motion and appeal is finally exhausted. Marvin Frankel, a former Federal District Court judge, believes that the fundamental reason lawyers are held in such low esteem is the role so many play as "hired guns." The public has "the vivid sense that we are not detached 'ministers of justice,' as people of the law might be in some utopia, but self-seeking shopkeepers whose wares are for sale."[56] The historic view was that a lawyer was an officer of the court and therefore an integral part of the scheme of justice. But the conception today is that of a paid servant of the client, justified in using any technical lever supplied by the law to advance the latter's interest. For in an adversary system the supposition is that, because the opposing interest is pulling an opposition set of levers, justice will somehow be done by the process itself in the resulting equilibrium. The aim of the individual advocate, however, is not justice but only victory.[57] This "hired gun" mentality was expressed with admirable terseness a few years ago by the hiring partner of a major Wall Street firm, who remarked to a third year law recruit that the "greatest thrill" in litigation "is to win when you're *wrong*."[58]

The dilemma posed by the "hired gun" mentality is obvious and it is one I sugggested earlier in this chapter: can an attorney be loyal to the traditional notions of lawyer-client privilege and of zealous advocacy, and at the same time remain a good and moral person?[59] Little help has come from the organized bar to deal with this dilemma, because, strange as it may seem to the laity, there is simply no agreement in the profession as to what conduct is "ethical" or "unethical." Ethics are said to be derived from experience, which is the embodiment of a society's practical wisdom and shared notions about the moral justification of individual and collective conduct. Legal codes are crystalizations of these notions and should, ideally at least, encourage a person to view his or her conduct through a moral prism. The fallacy of such codes, however, is that they always reflect the limited experience of individual attorneys and of the profession generally. Given the wide diversity of this experience, as well as its limitation, it is not surprising that many lawyers really do not recognize moral dilemmas when confronted with them, or have developed techniques to avoid or to rationalize them away.[60] One such technique we just mentioned: as an advocate in the adversary system a lawyer has no responsibility for outcomes; as long as each client is zealously represented, the system itself will take care of justice. Richard Wasserstrom calls another technique "role-differentiated behavior," and describes it thus:

> For where the attorney-client relationship exists, it is often appropriate and many times even obligatory for the attorney to do things that, all other things being equal, an ordinary person need not and should not do. What is characteristic of this role

of the lawyer is the lawyer's required indifference to a wide variety of ends and consequences that in other contexts would be of undeniable moral significance. . . . In this way the lawyer as professional comes to inhabit a simplified universe which is strikingly amoral—which regards as morally irrelevant any number of factors which non-professional citizens might take to be important, if not decisive, in their everyday lives.[61]

One feature of this simplified intellectual world is that it is often a very comfortable one to inhabit. Hence the general lack of concern to seek remedies for the double mindset we have been discussing. Whether or not this system only sometimes satisfies the national longing for justice, whether or not it works badly or well, the organized bar nevertheless seeks to preserve it. Geoffrey Hazard of Yale Law School has compared current efforts to fine-tune the legal system to "running a bucket brigade when you're dealing with tidal waves of social change." Charles Halpern, Dean of the new CUNY Law School, makes the same point: "The real problem is that the people closest to the system and most responsible for the problems are the people for whom the system works beautifully."[62] The huge costs and delays of the system have been readily acknowledged but little addressed. "Though doctors are learning to assess the costs and benefits of medical procedures and new technologies," observes Derek Bok, "lawyers are not making a comparable effort to evaluate provisions for appeal, for legal representation, for adversary hearings, or for other legal safeguards to see whether they are worth in justice what they cost in money and delay. . . . Nor has anyone done much to explore the forces that encourage or inhibit litigation so that we can better predict the rise and fall of legal activity."[63] The conclusion we must draw, then, is that, because of this double mindset conditioning the majority in the legal profession, the two great deficiencies of the profession itself, access and cost, will more than likely remain unaddressed, and continue to constitute a serious inhibiting factor for someone's pursuit of law as a vocation to justice and love.

VI

Up to now my concern has been to highlight the four major problem areas endemic to the functioning of America's legal culture. For these four areas also constitute the major obstacles that must eventually be faced and somehow grappled with by anyone who feels "called" as a lawyer to promote justice and love in society. How precisely these obstacles are to be overcome, however, is not all that clear. As I noted earlier, the legal profession expresses all too accurately those individualistic and material values cherished by most Americans. The freedom we prize so highly is very often conceived of as freedom to compete, acquire, and possess, a *laissez-faire* mentality that relegates shared responsibilities and communitarian purposes to secondary importance. An ethic of justice and love, on the other hand, at the very least conceives of freedom in terms of concern for the neighbor as well as for oneself, and tends to increase rather than decrease the scope of fellowship and community. When applied to American law such an ethic challenges at one and the same time the pragmatism of our legal tradition, the impersonality of our legal education, and the preoccupation of the profession itself with technique, conflict, and profit. What grounds for hope can there be for a lawyer that some good for individuals and society will result from this ethical challenge?

For those who believe in God, of course, the ultimate ground for hope will be religious. For they can be convinced that through a continuing creative and salvific action God is present somehow to all human experience, whether secular or sacred. From this point of view there is necessarily a religious dimension to all legal experience, whether or not individual attorneys have any awareness of this. That is to say, no human institution is an autonomous structure in which God has no interest, since every human institution influences the way people live in society, which in turn influences the way they think about God and their neighbor. Hence it will generally be easier to live a good life and to find God in a just society than in an unjust one. The fact that secular institutions are never found to be all good, that most are indeed ambiguous, a mix of good and bad, is simply a reflection of the human condition. Religious institutions are not all good either, but share this same ambiguity of all things human.

Thus the prior concern of the religious person in this sense is not what he or she should be doing in secular life, but what God might be doing. For before any human being pursues justice and love, God pursues them. Before any human being promotes freedom and equality, God does. Though ultimately the purpose of God's providential design is the union of all persons with God's own self in the sphere of the sacred, God's immediate purposes in the secular sphere must be secular, i.e. in conformity with the nature of a particular institution. These purposes God carries out through the meshing of divine providence with human prudence, through the instrumentality of men and women whose prudential judgments further any given providential design. Hence persons in the legal profession who believe in God can also believe not only that their "call" comes from God, but that finally there is hope for the improvement of their profession because God is already concerned with their concerns, and that any initiatives on their part constitute a collaboration with the divine initiatives already present.

But there are other and perhaps more immediate grounds for hope, and these come from the experience of "vocation" itself. Concretely this experience includes, it seems to me, the sense of a threefold mission and of one's being called to carry it out. The mission is one of technical competence, human concern, and social responsibility. The strength of one's hope will depend upon the depth of one's sensitivity and commitment. Let us summarize briefly the content and objectives of this threefold mission.

No lawyer can fulfill her or his vocation without first achieving a high degree of technical competence. I have emphasized at some length the risks involved in striving for such analytical rigor in the study and practice of the law. But unless one does strive for it, all talk about one's mission as an attorney to promote justice and love in society will be suspect. The problem is never with analytic skill as such, just as the problem is never with law as such. The risk is rather that the meaning of law will be reduced to technique, thereby restricting legal education to training in technique, and understanding legal practice as the use of technique to manipulate human behavior. More specifically, the problem at all three levels is the separation of technique from values. This was the theme of the 1984 American Bar Association conference on legal education. "Law plus X equals justice. X is the value system," said Judge Dorothy W. Nelson of the Ninth U.S. Circuit Court of Appeals. She was supported by Robert MacCrate, partner in the New York firm of Sullivan and Cromwell and member of the

American Bar Association Board of Governors: "Law schools must be more explicit in exploring the values underlying the law and its practice in order to assist those entering the practice and beyond to recognize and accept their responsibilities. We need a sense of what our values should be." Judge Robert E. Keeton of the U.S. District Court in Massachusetts and former associate dean of Harvard Law School was more explicit: "We are not talking about the value of skills training because of the skills learned. The deeper value is that it increases understanding of the legal system and the professional role. . . . You must experience the conflict of interest between two values."[64]

This perennial risk in law of separating technique from values should thus in no way obscure the importance of such technique to the professional as such. Karl Llewellyn once observed that technique without values is wickedness, but values without technique is foolishness. The aim is to become an accomplished technician without losing sight of the values of justice and love which the vocation is all about. This means that any lawyer has to spend a great deal of time in essentially boring endeavor, and that vast amounts of trivial detail can be mastered only with a lot of unrelieved drudgery. Grant Gilmore has put it well: "If it is your dream to slay the corporate dragon in his lair or to protect the environment against its predators, you will get nowhere unless you have accepted the harsh necessity of making yourself into at least as good a lawyer, on the nuts and bolts level, as the lawyers for the dragons and the predators, who will be very good indeed."[65]

The quest of law for justice is often limited by technique and sometimes even thwarted, but much more frequently the mastery of technique makes possible the success of this quest, since such mastery can engender suggestions of rightness that might otherwise not have presented themselves. Well developed analytical skills can thus be used to critique the consequences and meanings of certain legal actions and procedures, that is to say, to critique values in the law itself. Gilmore's colleague at Yale, Charles Black, once recalled a remark by a late professor of music at the University to the effect that the aim of all training in singing is that the student at last learn to sing naturally. "I profoundly believe," writes Black, "that the final result of training in law is that one may come close to thinking naturally about problems of justice. It is visibly true of law that a really high technical proficiency liberates instead of binds, and this is one of the surest diagnostic signs of art."[66]

Hence before anyone can even begin to think about how to deal as a lawyer with issues of justice and love, that person must first want to be a lawyer and to master the skills of the craft. This means that he or she must want to be part of the legal establishment. The power to influence society belongs to those who have gained recognized status among peers; radicals and mavericks tend in the long run to carry little weight in a profession. It is important to recognize, therefore, before we examine the lawyer's second mission, that, in spite of the obstacles acknowledged earlier, the legal profession is not devoid of interest in how law affects human lives. The profession's history and its ideals testify to law's humanistic base and to the underlying aspiration of lawyers to care for people. The problem with the profession is not ideals and aspiration but practice.

Legal education, as we saw, has been almost exclusively concerned with principles and logical analysis, and generally avoids what appears to be the quagmire of moral inquiry. While ethical and social responsibilities are readily recognized by the bar, lawyers tend to be inattentive to them in practice because such inattention has been nurtured in law school. Law school and law practice thus inevitably tend to distort the reality of the world of law by interpreting the legal process as simply a set of rules. Whereas in fact "the process consists in the interplay of the persons forming the rule with the persons applying it and the persons submitting to it."[67] To be "called" to the bar thus means to be called to a concern for persons in society, and in particular for the interpersonal relationships between lawyer and client.

The difficulty, of course, as Richard Wasserstrom has pointed out, is that lawyers in their professional role can at the same time be highly involved with a client's special interest and yet fail to view the client as a whole person, to be dealt with as an equal and treated with the respect and dignity deserved by an equal. One reason for this is the relationship of inequality that is in some sense, at least historically, intrinsic to all professionalism. By definition the lawyer possesses an expertise not easily attainable outside the profession. Along with this expertise goes a special language by which lawyers communicate with other lawyers but not with clients. Since communication is one distinguishing characteristic of persons, this fact helps make the client less than a person in the lawyer's eyes. The client has the added disadvantage of not really being able to evaluate how well or badly the lawyer is performing. Not clients but fellow professionals evaluate lawyers, since, unlike clients, they have the power to criticize and regulate effectively.

Finally, clients almost always have some serious life problem, and this tends to render them vulnerable and to induce dependence on lawyers for advice and wellbeing. This life problem in turn naturally leads the lawyer to see the client partially, to focus on that part of his or her person that can be altered, corrected, or otherwise assisted professionally. For all these reasons the lawyer-client relationship conspires to depersonalize clients in lawyers' eyes, and to foster responses to them that are manipulative and paternalistic. Such responses constitute that "role-differentiated behavior" referred to earlier, behavior which can have great appeal for lawyers, who find it much easier to deal with clients as objects than as persons. Whether an individual client is actually dealt with as an object will therefore depend on whether a lawyer has so internalized this kind of professional role that it has become the dominant role in life, or whether he or she has been able to keep this role at a certain distance and in perspective, in order to minimize its bad consequences without destroying the good that high professional competence can achieve.[68]

To fulfill a legal mission of human concern, then, a lawyer has to understand and practice legal skills not just within the context of a legal problem but also in the context of a human life. There has to be some focus upon the human condition as well as upon technical mastery. For in touching a legal problem this mastery also and inevitably touches a total life situation, a fact that can be ignored by the attorney only at the price of ignoring vocation and mission. Thomas Shaffer calls such concern an "ethics of care," an orientation governed by "an aspiration to *care* for the client and to be cared for by him. It admits that the law-office conversation is moral and that those who speak to one another in law offices are interdependent and at risk. It aspires to moral discourse as an exercise of love. . . . The risk of openness is a risk involving the person of the client, and acceptance of the principle (and of the fact) that . . . it is not only an argument or interest being asserted but a person and a relationship being lived."[69] Inequality, in other words, is not necessarily intrinsic to professionalism.

One consequence of this ethics of care is the need for a lawyer to know something about the techniques for being open, for being sensitive to what in fact worries clients, not just what ought to worry them. "He will learn to listen to what his client says, attend to what his client feels, find out about the client's values. . . . Law students would come to insist on education which trains them in the skills of sincerity, congruence, and acceptance."[70] Within such an ethical framework adversarial skills are not necessarily more valuable than those of counsellor, counciliator, and compromiser. For society needs lawyers at home not only in conflict but also in arbitration, ombudsmanship, mediation and negotiation. "We tend to forget," said Chief Justice Burger to the American Bar Association, "that we ought to be healers, healers of conflicts. Doctors, in spite of astronomical medical costs, still retain a high degree of public confidence because they are perceived as healers. Should lawyers not be healers? Healers, not warriors? Healers, not procurers? Healers, not hired guns?"[71]

Perhaps a more important consequence of commitment to an ethics of care is the likelihood that a lawyer's concept of justice will be effectively modified. I cited earlier Derek Bok's critique of the dangerous mindset of most successful attorneys, one aspect of which is their willingness to think of justice in purely procedural terms, as being constituted exclusively by fair procedure and due process. Attentiveness to the total life of the client as a human person, however, will inevitably tend to push the concept of justice back from its public administration to its private source in interpersonal relationships. This is much closer to the biblical idea of the "just person"; it calls upon impulses to cooperation and friendship, not on impulses to assert rights, demand duties, or threaten force. In this sense the just relationship is synonymous with the loving relationship, the model being the love of God for his people. Such a concept is also very close to the biblical concept of "covenant," understood as a relationship of fidelity and mutual understanding. Such fidelity implies good faith, counsel, character, and trust. Hence the lawyer who truly listens to clients, who can empathize, who can pick up the unspoken feelings of participants in painful situations, is not only the person to whom people will confide and share their deepest experiences, he or she is also a lawyer who fulfills in a special way a vocation to justice and love.[72]

This ethics of individual care parallels closely an ethics of social responsibility which characterizes the third mission of the legal profession, namely care for the social order. Even though as a group they are reluctant to admit it, lawyers have more to do with the direction society takes than any other profession. We just discussed the power they have over clients that comes from superior training, knowledge, and skill, but their capacity to influence human life in business, government, and local communities is far greater, and their corresponding responsibility to use this power for good is both heavy and constitutive of the lawyer's vocation.[73] While the actual work of most lawyers is restricted to private practice, the legal profession itself functions as a crucial interactive structure in society. Whether it acts to obstruct, stabilize, or reform the social order, it acts always as an instrument of social change.

"Organization," claims Harvard's Paul Freund, "is inextricably bound up with larger social patterns. Indeed, if there is a seamless web with regard to the legal profession it is just here, in its relationship to the economic, educational, and political systems. . . . The distinctive role of the legal profession is to serve as the architect of structure and process."[74] The issue, of course, is what goals in society does the architect have? Every society is constituted by what Robert MacIver has called a "firmament of law," which represents to the world that particular order that constitutes the life-context of a people. This "cultural meaning of law," however, to use Douglas Sturm's phrase, is seldom discussed by lawyers, even by those who are judges, policy-makers, and legislators. Yet the power they have to influence their culture is enormous, and if an ethics of social responsibility does not govern their professional lives, then this power will inevitably tend to corrupt, as all power does.

In a recent study of American law, Lawrence M. Friedman of Stanford University develops the theme that law is both a product and a catalyst for social change. This capacity of law to mirror as well as to give form to society, he argues, explains why the humanistic study of law provides a unique vantage point for viewing the culture of which it is a part. Legal realism, of course, supports this argument: if one seriously takes into account all the elements in a given cultural situation, it is much easier to see what is called for by way of social change. Recent changes in our penal law, for example, especially the death penalty, reflect a general modern tendency to place much greater reliance on deadly force as a means of overcoming our frustration with crime. I share the dismay of many regarding this use of the death penalty, but it is indeed part of a tendency that seems also to be reflected in recent international policy. Yet these harsher penalties, once solidified into statutory law, inevitably condition for years to come the humane character of American society as well as how Americans in general view criminals as persons.[75] Hence to be adequately practiced, law must be understood contextually, not in autonomous isolation as legal realists and positivists would claim. For, as we saw earlier, such a drive for the uniqueness of law only serves to support the dominant American ethic of competitive individualism, and to absolve the legal profession from seeing itself as an inevitable part of a more inclusive pattern of social interaction. Law simply cannot be isolated from all other means of articulating a social ethos.[76]

Openly recognizing in their public lives this contextual character of law is the first and perhaps most effective way for lawyers to realize their mission of social responsibility. Such recognition may well place them squarely against the mainstream of current legal thinking on the subject, but it will also enable them to evaluate the broader implications of the legal "system" and its norms. As practitioners they will still occupy specific places in this system, but their sense of larger meanings will inevitably influence both the places they choose and the correctives to the system they elect to apply. If their work is in the adversary arena, for example, they will sense an obligation to society as well as to clients, and when there is a clear conflict between the two, this conflict will not necessarily be resolved by winning for the client. "There is a vast difference," said Cornell's Roger Cramton, then president of the Association of American Law Schools, "between the morally upright lawyer and the lawyer who conforms to the needs of the client and does anything to that end if it does not break the law. Total commitment to the client's cause pushes the lawyer toward amoral if not immoral acts. . . . Protecting the criminal defendant against the state is one thing, but maximizing the gain of a private corporation or individual is another. . . . A narrow focus that rests on the nuts and bolts of making a client win shows a lack of such civilizing qualities as trust and compassion. The result is not justice but social disaster."[77]

Cramton's call for more responsible patterns of advocacy highlights the continuing need for self-criticism by the organized bar. This need is so urgent because every aspect of the legal profession is today under public scrutiny, from access, cost, and complexity to the overcrowding of courts and the oversupply of lawyers. People rightfully question whether the recent rapid growth in the number of lawyers has in fact been for the common good. The public has a right to know, for example, why fairly obvious areas of law, such as divorce, probate, and personal injury cannot be simplified and access to courts made easier and less expensive. Yet change continues to be resisted, no-fault insurance being the only example of any significant development in these areas.

There is also understandable concern about the extent to which members of the profession serve the poor in our society. The alarming announcement in 1982 by the Census Bureau that 15 percent of all Americans were living below the poverty line, combined with the severe underfunding of the Legal Services Corporation and even threats of its abolition by the Reagan administration,[78] make an increase in responsibility for such voluntary service imperative. One example of such responsibility is a program organized in 1984 by the New York City Bar Association in which 30 of the largest firms and 20 corporate law departments pledged to devote 30 hours a year per lawyer to public service work, primarily to civil cases involving fraud, landlord-tenant matters, and the wrongful denial of government benefits. But this program will involve only 5,000 of the City's 45,000 lawyers, and marks a very belated attempt to comply with the requirement of the Code of Professional Responsibility that all lawyers "participate or otherwise support provision of legal services to the disadvantaged." In 1980 this same Bar Association overwhelmingly rejected a two-year study by one of its own special committees, that proposed making 30 to 50 hours of public interest activity mandatory.

In underlining this need for a critical rethinking of the profession's functioning in society I do not wish to imply that law has not greatly benefited the public sphere in recent years. The remarkable advances in civil rights law, poverty law, family law, environmental law, and consumer protection law testify to our country's capacity for innovation and vigorous response

to pressing claims for social justice. But all these laws are em-
bodiments of values held by those who promoted, supported,
and enacted them at a particular point in history. What has
to be addressed now is our own point in history. If lawyers
are to be true to their mission of social responsibility, they must
be alert to the ever new demands being made on their profession, and in constant search for values and tactics needed for
response. What, for example, will be one's position as a lawyer
on the key moral issue of our time, namely the value of human
life? The Supreme Court's abortion and death penalty cases
raise this issue in specifically legal terms. Upon what value
sources will the lawyer draw to respond to this very public
question of who is a member of the human community?[79]

Because lawyers guard our justice system in ever larger
numbers, they must inevitably become more implicated in such
public issues and forced to shoulder ever greater responsibility for the public weal. And here once again we encounter the
relation of justice to love. For love, understood as agape, that
force in human life which unites persons in the public as well
as in the private spheres, is capable of energizing the lawyer's
professional work so that it has meaning and direction for the
larger human community. This same legal activity, on the other
hand, is essential for love to have some structure in society.
For without the various branches of law that bring order to
such areas as property, personal injuries, contracts, family obligations, criminal acts, and public administration, love would
be forced to operate in social chaos. Of itself law is constitutive
neither of justice nor of love, but both of these forces need law
and lawyers to become operative in a nation's life.[80] The laws
of society often work against love, of course, and sometimes
even against justice, but this only highlights all the more the
need for lawyers dedicated to both virtues, as well as to making them visible in the institutions of society as a whole.

I began by asking what grounds there were for hoping that
some good for individuals and society will come from meeting the four challenges from our national character, our legal
tradition, our law schools, and the organized bar. I want to
end with a word of caution in regard to the grounds for hope
that I have drawn from the lawyer's threefold mission: these
grounds must be relied upon primarily for courage, not success. In using law to shape one's world, one is using no blunt
instrument but one of extraordinary delicacy and precision.

Such use is therefore an art, not at all the science that Langdell envisioned. For the legal system as such is imperfect, "flawed," to use Derek Bok's word, and the results of its operation are very often unpredictable. This means that at any given moment law presents a set of possibilities, more or less likely to occur, the likelihood of occurrence being conditioned by human intuition, decision, and purpose. According to Charles Black, the central problem of this art of law is that of finding and using the openings provided by these possibilities. Black is worth quoting at length:

> The art of law is founded upon and practiced within a set of tensions between aims not simultaneously realizable in full. On the one hand the aim of attaining justice . . . and on the other hand the aim of using the authority of law in a legitimate manner, employing but not straining the techniques sanctioned as legitimate within our legal culture. Living and working within this tension is not made the more easy by the fact that no reasoning about justice or even about practicability, and no reasoning about legal legitimacy, can ever be altogether demonstrated, like a demonstration in mathematics or even in physical science. What can be asked of the artist in law is . . . that he continually explore, with disciplined imagination, the means to justice within the legal system, and that at the same time he be continually responsive to the demand for reasoned justification within that system. The continued search for creative resolution of this tension is one of the main things the art of law is about.[81]

To encounter this tension creatively in one's life as a lawyer, however, will usually result neither in success nor in failure but more often in ambiguity. Black cites a remark by Sir Joshua Reynolds to the effect that the look of reality in painting results from showing a clear line when the line is clear and not showing a clear line when the line is not clear, and then notes that one of the central problems constantly recurring in the art of law is the problem of clarity and certainty. "I sought for certainty," writes Benjamin Cardozo of his first years as a judge. "I was oppressed and disheartened when I found that the quest for it was futile. . . . As the years have gone by, and as I have reflected more and more upon the nature of the judicial process, I have become reconciled to the uncertainty, because I have grown to see it as inevitable."[82] Lawyers "called" to a threefold mission must therefore become reconciled to uncertainty and to unclear lines. Nor should they be disheartened by the ambiguity they find in the art of doing justice, because this art in some sense is also a way of loving, and nothing is more ambiguous than human love.

Hence besides hope and courage, such lawyers need to make an act of faith as well. This means faith in something greater than law itself, for if law is the ultimate morality and religion of the lawyer, then private interests will inevitably prevail in the profession and concern for the public good will wane. To practice law as a vocation is thus to embody the truth of one's faith in actions that overcome doubts and lead to political vision. It is also to fly blind, to approximate justice, and to wait with patience for the gift of love. Because disillusion is the great risk, the ambiguity of law itself must somehow become an object of faith and hope and a source of courage. Grant Gilmore sensed this when he wrote: "Law, like a radioactive substance, renews itself through a process of continual decay. The disease which threatens to destroy the *corpus juris* sets in motion the antibodies which enable it to survive."[83]

5

The Risk
of Moral Consensus

In this chapter I want to focus on the phenomenon of public anger and the rhetoric of moral indignation to which it gives rise. The danger of any such anger, even if justified, is that it may be managed by government not to secure the common good of the nation, but to achieve purposes that are narrowly political and to produce results altogether out of proportion to the cause. One example of such a phenomenon, which clearly determined the outcome of the First World War, is the anger provoked in this country by Germany's sinking of a British passenger liner in May 1915. It was a tragedy in which all the dangers inherent in national outrage were fully realized. This 1915 event has been exhaustively researched, and the rich documentation now enables us to evaluate all its components, legal, political, and moral, with thoroughness and from a vantage point denied to its contemporaries. Dipping into this history will, I think, prove to be both fascinating and instructive.

On the afternoon of May 7, 1915, the British passenger liner *Lusitania* was torpedoed by a German submarine off the Irish coast and sank within eighteen minutes. With it went the lives of almost 1,200 people, 128 of whom were Americans. In the United States the news caused so tremendous a sensation that not only Americans but people throughout the world wondered whether it meant war. Public indignation against Germany reached a white heat and diplomatic repercussions were momentous. "The position taken by the United States on the *Lusitania* case ultimately determined American intervention, the outcome of the war, and the fate of Europe."[1] The regicides of Louis XVI are said to have looked at the whole French Revolution through the tiny window of his guillotine. After

May 7, 1915 all German-American relations seem to have been conducted through the narrow portholes of the *Lusitania*.

In its diplomatic notes to Berlin, Washington sought to place squarely upon the German Government full accountability for the ruthless murder of helpless men, women, and children. The British historian Colin Simpson believes this American position to have been at best legally unsound and at worst motivated by dishonesty and fraud.[2] His evidence locates accountability for the great loss of life only minimally in the German torpedo. He assigns a certain share to the faulty design of the ship itself, much more to its contraband and explosive cargo, and most of all to the prior decisions and their subsequent concealment by British Admiralty personnel.

The historical record shows that all of this was known at the time by Washington but was deliberately concealed from the people. Had it been publicly known, of course, much of the seething anger of the country would have been muted, and its usefulness to Washington severely curtailed. Hence the issue to be explored, in the context of the public virtue of public officials, is the accountability of President Wilson and his advisors. In his official statements Wilson gave eloquent voice to the nation's moral outrage. He branded submarine attacks without warning against unarmed passenger vessels as "crime against humanity," and demanded that Germany disavow the *Lusitania* sinking and give up all such deeds in the future. While he continually insisted upon the illegality of such attacks under existing rules of warfare, it is clear that what he sought was to control the use of this new weapon not by law but by an appeal to national conscience. Nor can there be any doubt about his willingness to go to war if Germany would not accept America's moral consensus. The point is whether Wilson had any right to speak in this way when he protested this particular sinking. For, as we shall see, he was neither on firm ground legally, nor did he ever take into full account all the facts and circumstances of the tragedy as he actually knew them.

I

Until February 1915, Wilson's foreign policy in regard to the European war had been relatively uncomplicated: England controlled the seas, Germany dominated the continent, and the United States tried to accept and adapt to a stalemated situation which as yet offered little threat of American involvement. Wilson thus made no protest against the German invasion of Belgium, in spite of his country's moral indignation and his personal sympathy for the Allied cause. He likewise adapted as best he could to England's constant violation of our neutral shipping rights as a result of its decision in November 1914 to blockade the whole of the North Sea. The points of friction in Anglo-American relations in this area were in fact serious, and were recognized as such by the British Foreign Office. But Wilson grudgingly accommodated himself to these illegalities. While he was influenced no doubt by the sudden economic prosperity of the country as a result of munitions traffic with the Allies, there seems to be general agreement that his primary motivation was a desire to promote an early peace in Europe and a belief that any breach of good diplomatic relations with England would prevent his playing the role of peacemaker. He was well aware, he said in December 1914, that the origins of the war were complex and that Germany was not alone responsible. Any decisive victory would thus bring danger of an unjust peace, whereas early deadlock would show the futility of employing force as a means of resolving differences.[3]

Substantial changes in this policy began in February 1915, when Germany retaliated against the British blockade by using an untried weapon, the submarine. Since the German surface fleet was immobilized, the success of the submarine against vessels of war made naval officers consider its employment as a destroyer of commerce. Few technical obstacles stood in the way, but serious legal questions arose at once. According to old and well established rules of warfare, a belligerent warship might be sunk at sight, but a merchantman might not be attacked without determining whether she was enemy or neutral, or destroyed without providing for the safety of her passengers and crew. In late 1914, accordingly, submarines were ordered to attack merchant vessels under the rules of warfare and to report on the practicality of this procedure. Though U-boats sank several vessels in a legal manner, their commanders reported that the stream of commerce to England and the continent could be checked only by disregarding the rules.[4] The German Government therefore began to consider a more widespread submarine campaign, weighing its military possibilities, legal justification, and political expediency. The Foreign Office, well aware that neutrals would challenge the policy, insisted that Germany could not embark upon it without giving a public warning to neutrals to avoid the zone of operations. It is this public warning on February 2nd which occasioned the American reply of February 10th containing the ominous phrase "strict accountability."

Germany's declaration was an attempt to win toleration for the ruthless expedient of a nation inferior to her enemy on the seas:

> For her violations of international law Great Britain pleads the vital interest which the British Empire has at stake, and neutral powers seem to satisfy themselves with theoretical protest. Therefore in fact they accept the vital interests of belligerents as sufficient excuse for every method of warfare. Germany must now appeal to these same vital interests to its regret. . . . Just as England has designated the area between Scotland and Norway as an area of war, so Germany now declares all water surrounding Great Britain and Ireland including the entire English Channel as an area of war, and thus proceeds against the shipping of the enemy.

Sometimes it might not be possible, the declaration continued, to safeguard persons and cargoes on enemy ships, and while Germany would make every effort to spare neutral vessels, the neutral flag could not be accepted as conclusive of character since the British frequently used the flags of neutral countries. The note ended:

> The German Government. . . . may expect that neutral powers will show no less consideration for the vital interests of Germany than for those of England and will aid in keeping their citizens and the property of the latter from this area.[5]

The American reply to this totally unexpected turn of events was actually intended by Wilson to be friendly as well as firm. There were at the time no points of friction between the two governments. He understood well enough how the Germans could feel driven to extreme measures, nor was there any reason as yet for him to protest against submarine attacks upon Allied shipping. What concerned him primarily just now were American neutral rights. Using a draft submitted by Robert Lansing, Counselor to the State Department, he typed the final note on his own typewriter. Since there was no international law governing the use of submarines as far as neutrals were concerned, he and Lansing had to work within the accepted rules. To sink vessels without warning, the President said, would be an act unprecedented in naval warfare. If a German submarine

> should destroy on the high seas an American vessel or the lives of American citizens, it would be difficult for the Government of the United States to view the act in any other light than as an indefensible violation of neutral rights. . . .
>
> If such a deplorable situation should arise, the Imperial German Government can readily appreciate that the Government of the United States would be constrained to hold the Imperial German Government to a strict accountability for such acts of the naval authorities and to take any steps it might be necessary to take to safeguard American lives and property and to secure to American citizens the full enjoyment of their acknowledged rights on the high seas.[6]

There was loud alarm in the Wilhelmstrasse when this note arrived, and the German reply of February 16th gave a very sweeping guarantee that ships flying the American flag would not be subject to underseas attack. At the same time it tried to underline, in fairly temperate language, three obstacles which Germany faced in trying to honor the just rights of neutrals: the arming of British merchantmen, the English use of the American flag, and the orders issued to British captains regarding resistance to submarines.[7] Each of these factors is extremely important in understanding the legal difficulties of the next step in Wilson's developing policy, and they will repay our closer scrutiny at this point.

The law of nations had long recognized the right of a merchant ship to carry defensive armament, of limited number and calibre, which would protect it from enemy cruisers but prevent it from conducting offensive operations. In September 1914 the British government gave as its justification for arming merchantmen the necessity of a defense against Germany's arming merchant vessels as commerce destroyers. It contended that a belligerent merchantman which carried armament for defense did not acquire the character of a public ship of war, and was not restricted by the ordinary rules governing such vessels. By the beginning of 1915, however, the danger from armed German merchant ships had disappeared and was followed by the emergence of the U-boat. The British soon discovered that a five or six inch gun could easily sink a submarine, and accordingly ordered their merchantmen to destroy any U-boat that came within range. A submarine would thus be in peril if it stopped a merchant ship armed for "defense" in order to go through the usual formula of "visit and search." The question which pressed for an answer, therefore, was whether under these conditions a merchant ship carrying defensive armament should be considered an armed public vessel, which under international law could be sunk at sight.

The Netherlands actually took such a position in August 1914, maintaining that the distinction between offensive and defensive armament was obsolete, and excluding from Dutch ports all belligerent ships that were in any way armed. This was an unprecedented interpretation of neutral duties, however, and found only sporadic support in Washington. There the legal question was left unanswered, although Wilson was quite aware of it. In April 1915, after the *Falaba* was sunk (which we shall consider presently), he asked his Secretary of State, William J. Bryan, to consider the following:

> If *some* British merchantships were known to be armed and the British Government had in fact authorized or advised all merchantmen to arm themselves against submarines, and assuming it to have been impracticable for the German commander to ascertain whether the *Falaba* was armed, was he justified in the circumstances in acting upon the theory that the British authorization had in effect transformed all British merchantmen into public armed vessels and made them liable to an attack as such?[8]

A second obstacle to legal use of the submarine was the use of the American flag by the British. The *Lusitania* herself hoisted the American flag to hide her identity when she neared the Irish coast on February 5th, and other ships misused neutral flags in order to attack submarines. Since U-boat commanders found it dangerous to approach neutral ships in a legal manner, they tended more and more to ignore legality. An occasional use of the neutral flag as a *ruse de guerre* was of course valid, but general misuse of neutral flags in dangerous waters would inevitably jeopardize all neutral shipping. Protests by Washington to London on this question were never very strong and, after occasioning a polite diplomatic reassurance, were regularly ignored.[9]

The third obstacle was deliberate attacks upon submarines by British merchantmen. On February 10, 1915, the British Admiralty issued the following orders to masters of merchant ships: "If a submarine comes up suddenly close ahead of you with obvious hostile intention, steer straight at her at your utmost speed altering course as necessary to keep her ahead." When the German Government learned of this, it presented its grievance to the Department of State, adding the fact that the British had offered a large sum of money for the destruction of the first German submarine by a British merchantman. The German Foreign Office maintained, not without reason, that in view of such orders it was suicidal for Germany to conform to international law in its submarine warfare. Since British ships were ordered to attack before a U-boat could possibly give the prescribed warning, it would seem that *ipso facto* they became warships subject to destruction without warning. By early March the award offered by the Admiralty had in fact been claimed by three British ships, and shortly afterwards several captains were decorated for ramming submarines.[10]

The German note of February 10th, which spoke of these three obstacles, raises in retrospect a difficult diplomatic question: Could the United States, while claiming neutrality, legitimately insist upon a change in the rules of cruiser warfare which would give an enormous advantage to Germany? In 1916 Lansing, then Secretary of State, actually proposed that Wilson advocate such a change, but in early 1915 no one could seriously consider it. Neither Wilson nor his advisors wanted to champion the German cause against England. What alarmed them about the submarine announcement was that its implementation might mean an American ship actually sunk (not merely stopped, searched, and delayed as with the British) and, above all, American lives lost. Accommodation to *this* type of neutral rights violation could not be carried off with the same delayed reckoning policy employed toward British violations. Hence the importance of making it clear that the consequences would involve a "strict accountability." The stern American tone in fact worked. Germany gave assurances that no American ship would be attacked and this was satisfactory at the time. The question of the legality of Germany's use of the submarine against her enemies' shipping was something the belligerents might settle among themselves.

II

In this first German-American exchange over the submarine a very thorny legal problem was never mentioned: What claim could Washington make, under the cruiser rules then in force, for the rights and lives of American citizens on belligerent ships? Wilson's note to Germany spoke only of "an American vessel or the lives of American citizens," and of safeguarding "American lives and property." Was a clear distinction between American ships and those of belligerents omitted deliberately, in order to take advantage of the ambiguity in later negotiations? This is not impossible, of course, but there is no evidence for it, and documents immediately subsequent speak only of American vessels.[11] Nevertheless, the ambiguity was there: What precisely was to be the full content of "strict accountability?" An answer was suddenly demanded when a submarine halted the British cargo and passenger liner *Falaba*, gave its captain twenty minutes to abandon ship, then fired a torpedo because of the sudden appearance of an armed British trawler. The munitions in the cargo exploded and one American, Leon Thrasher, lost his life. This occasioned sharp debate between Bryan and Lansing over the formulation of a proper response.

The Secretary of State was profoundly disturbed by the event, because he saw a danger of war unless we clearly limited the meaning of "strict accountability." He argued that the American Government should recognize that the German measures, while illegal in themselves, were retaliation for acts of Germany's enemies which were equally illegal, and that, having accommodated itself to one set of violations, it was bound to seek accommodation with the other. He demanded that "strict" accountability should not be interpreted as "immediate" accountability, but that the final reckoning should be deferred, as was being done with England. The crux of his argument was that an American, by embarking on a belligerent ship after a warning of the danger, could not impose upon his government an obligation to obtain an indemnity for a loss which due diligence might have avoided. He consequently urged Wilson to warn American citizens against travelling on belligerent ships, strongly maintaining that it was a self-evident rule of law that they incurred the risks of their location. "If the arming of merchant vessels," he said, "so changes their character as to affect the rights of those who travel on them, the risks assumed by an American passenger would necessarily be greatly increased and he might occupy the position of a foreigner who goes into a fortified city, or exposes himself when a battle is on."[12] In view of the contrary position of Lansing below, it is worth noting the support for Bryan given by two authorities on international law:

> Had the United States confined itself to protesting the possible destruction of American vessels or human beings on American vessels, its position would have been legally privileged and probably unexceptionable. . . . There was no precedent or legal warrant for a neutral to protect a *belligerent* ship from attack by its enemy because it happened to have on board American citizens. The exclusive jurisdiction of the country of the vessel's flag, to which all on board are subject, is an unchallengeable rule of law. By failing to observe it the United States went out of its way to court trouble.[13]

Lansing argued for a very different interpretation of the February 10th note, asserting that an American taking passage on a belligerent merchantman had the right to assume that the rules of naval warfare would be observed. To take a position that Thrasher would have kept out of the war zone "would amount to an admission of Germany's right to perform lawless acts in that area." Admitting all the time that a desire to keep out of war would favor adopting Bryan's policy, he nonetheless urged that national dignity and duty demanded holding Germany to "strict accountability for every American life lost by submarine attack on the high seas." Moreover, the legality of the method employed to sink the *Falaba* could not be debated, for "debating the legality to destroy life and the legality to destroy property are very different things." The Counselor thus made his own the distinction between attacks on life and attacks on property which were then current in the national press: the former outraged humanity, the latter affronted only international law. He quoted an opinion of the Joint State and Navy Neutrality Board that attacks against merchant vessels without warning were "not only illegal but revoltingly inhuman."[14]

Faced during the entire month of April with the barrage of conflicting advice, Wilson in the end could not decide on the content of a protest. We know that he still recognized the advantages of allowing Germany and England to settle the matter of the submarine between them. Bryan gave him a good basis for doing this: hold Germany "strictly accountable" only for the illegal destruction of life on American vessels and warn Americans against travelling on belligerent ships. We know too that he was deeply affected by the Secretary's arguments. In fact he seems to have decided at an April 27th Cabinet meeting to make no protest at all. Nevertheless, he did wish to make a protest. The problem was that he did not want to base it on legal grounds because these were evidently not strong enough to deal with what had gradually become for him the fundamental issue, namely the protection of all noncombatant life on the high seas. Just after mid-April he suggested to Bryan the type of note he would have liked to send on the *Falaba*. The last phrase especially indicates how concerned he now was to base his position on some kind of moral consensus:

> My idea, as you will see, is to put the whole note on very high grounds, – not on the loss of this single man's life, but on the interests of mankind which are involved and which Germany has always stood for; on the mainfest impropriety of a single mistake in employing an instrument against her enemy's commerce which it is impossible to employ in that use in accordance with any rules *that the world is likely to be willing to accept*.[15]

During this second stage of the submarine question, then, Wilson became convinced that there was a moral principle involved which had to be vindicated. This was now to be the objective of his policy on the submarine. If its pursuit meant the danger of hostilities with Germany, he told Bryan, this "ought not to alter our course so long as we think ourselves on the firm ground of right."[16] To a conference of the Methodist Church earlier in April he said he was then considering those "eternal principles of justice and righteousness" which lay behind government as well as church, and were the standards by which nations as well as men are judged. All his biographers agree that this was ultimately a religious ideal, originating in his strong Calvinist background, and that in foreign affairs it meant the subordination of immediate goals to superior ethical standards. One authority notes, however, that his faith "in the inevitable triumph of righteousness sometimes caused him to make illusory appraisals of the situations at hand and to devise quixotic or unworkable solutions." Too much introspective concern about the standards of right conduct also brought the danger of Pharisaism, "which was revealed, among other things, in Wilson's assumption that his motives and purposes were purer than those of the men with whom he happened to be contending."[17]

This introspection brought an even greater danger in May 1915: the idealist consulting his own spirit may find there the most determined purposes but rarely all the facts in any given situation. As we shall see, the *Lusitania* gave Wilson the occasion to articulate a set of values which embodied the very highest ideals of human conduct, but which could be successfully applied to the case at hand only by ignoring facts or conniving at their concealment. "[C]ertain important facts most directly connected with the sinking of the *Lusitania* may have escaped the attention of the United States," suggested Germany.[18] And a weary Bryan vainly protested in the midst of the controversy: "If a question is raised as to the correctness of the assumed facts, I can see no reason why we should refuse to consider the question of facts."[19] We have already noted the willingness to ignore obstacles to legal use of the submarine pointed out in the German note of February 16th. In the same way Wilson apparently assigned no weight at all to the key fact advanced by Bryan during April: to allow United States citizens to travel on belligerent ships, without a warning that they did so at their own peril, was openly to invite new crisis situations. We had no legal basis for guaranteeing Thrasher's safety on the *Falaba*. Not to say so by a warning was to encourage other Americans to run needless risks and tacitly to give to "strict accountability" a content not originally intended.

By the end of the month, however, Wilson was convinced that such a warning would distract from the real issue, which was that Germany had no right to cause another crisis like the *Falaba* by torpedoing a passenger liner at sight. At no time did he argue against the legality of Bryan's effort to limit this larger issue. The problem was that such limitation would inevitably weaken the moral position Wilson wanted to take. In the aftermath of the *Lusitania*, when America's second note was being drafted in early June, he admitted to Bryan: "I am inclined to think that we ought to take steps, as you suggest, to prevent our citizens from travelling on ships carrying munitions of war. . . . I am sorry to say that, study as I may the way to do it without hopelessly weakening our protest, I cannot find a way. . . ."[20] The rejection of Bryan's plea in the *Falaba* case is thus a crucial factor in the ultimate dénouement. This began to unfold at 1:35 on the afternoon of May 7th, when Captain

Turner altered the *Lusitania's* course toward Queenstown and headed it all unknowingly straight toward its chance encounter with Kapitän-Leutnant Schwieger's U-boat.

There is every reason to believe that Wilson experienced deep emotional shock when news of the sinking reached him later that same afternoon. After one dispatch tears were seen in his eyes. When the heavy loss of life was confirmed in the evening, he suddenly went out the main door of the White House and walked a long time, seemingly oblivious of the rain which was falling. He talked to no one and slept little that night. The next two and a half days he spent in seclusion. His private secretary recalls him saying at one point, "If I pondered over those tragic items about the *Lusitania* I should see red in everything. . . . In God's name how could any nation calling itself civilized have proposed so horrible a thing?" And one biographer notes that this was by far the severest testing that he had ever known: "The time was at hand when he must make decisions that would affect the whole course of the war . . . . He had to voice the moral judgment of the American people upon an international crime."[21] He was well aware that public opinion had been jolted as by no other event of the war. *The New York Times* gave the story six solid pages of coverage on the first day. Editorials blazed with indignation: the sinking was a "wholesale murder" and a "useless slaughter" with no mitigating circumstances. Nevertheless, what they urged upon the government was not an act of hostility toward Germany but a protest against the savagery of the act. It was this moral consensus of the country which Wilson was now determined to use in order to outlaw the submarine entirely.

III

With a high sense of his mission the President began at once to work upon an official note to Germany, apparently consulting with neither Cabinet members nor State Department officials. The first communication from Bryan on the afternoon of May 9th must therefore have been an occasion of some irritation, since it pointed out a disturbing fact: according to the Collector of Customs in New York almost the entire cargo of the *Lusitania* was contraband, including thousands of boxes of cartridges containing millions of rounds of ammunition. Should ships carrying such dangerous cargo be allowed to carry passengers? "Germany has a right to prevent contraband going to the allies and a ship carrying contraband should not rely upon passengers to protect her from attack—it would be like putting women and children in front of an army."[22] The telephone call to New York on May 8th, which had asked for this official information on munitions, was undoubtedly prompted by Bryan's April 26th conversation with George Viereck, editor of *The Fatherland*. He had seen the ammunition waiting on the pier to be loaded, he said, and he also showed Bryan previous *Lusitania* manifests proving that on all but one voyage the liner had carried similar cargo. Very likely Bryan mentioned these facts to the President, since they would have supported his position on the warning of Americans. We know the two had long discussions together on the evening of May 3rd and the morning of May 4th, and that Bryan at the time was deeply apprehensive about recent, and apparently mistaken, submarine attacks on two American tankers.[23]

Once this issue was raised by Bryan again, in the context of the *Lusitania* disaster, it had to be addressed. The precise question was the relevance of a munitions cargo for the warning of Americans off belligerent ships. The related questions of the legality of such a cargo and its possible explosion (resulting in the suddenness of the sinking and the great loss of life) do not seem to have become problems for Wilson until early June, after the charge of exploding munitions was officially made by Germany and insinuated in many of the published eyewitness accounts. Lansing was the first to address the present issue:

> Dear Mr. Secretary: I have been thinking over your suggestion that it might be considered that Americans, taking passage in a British vessel bound for a British port and passing through the German "war zone," did so, in a measure at least, at their own peril and, therefore, were not entitled to the full protection of this government. . . .
>
> After carefully considering the suggestion, I am convinced that this Government is in no position to adopt this view. To accept it would be to admit that the Government of the United States failed in its duty to its own citizens and permitted them to run risks without attempting to prevent them from doing so.
>
> It is my opinion in view of the facts that it would cause general public condemnation and indignant criticism in this

country, if the Government should attempt now to avoid vigorous action by asserting that the Americans drowned by the torpedoing of the *Lusitania* were blamable in having taken passage on that vessel. They had the right to expect a warning from their Government if it considered that it would not support them if they took risks by going abroad on British vessels.[24]

Wilson found this argument "unanswerable." Rather than admit he may have failed in his duty earlier, he preferred to avoid a warning now and so suppress the admission. "*Even if it were just* to take the position," he finally wrote Bryan on May 11th, "that a warning that an unlawful and outrageous thing would be done might operate as an exemption from responsibility on the part of those who issued it, so far as our citizens were concerned, it is now too late to take it. We defined our position at the outset and cannot alter it—at any rate so far as it affects the past."[25]

Having disposed of this issue, Wilson could finish the draft of his protest, which was finally sent to Germany on May 13th, after incorporating some suggestions from Bryan and Lansing. Very clear at the start was its assumption that the phrase of February 10th, "strict accountability," had referred all along to the protection of Americans on belligerent ships. It then went on to state what Wilson saw to be the fundamental issue, namely the protection of all noncombatant life on the high seas and the outlawing of the submarine altogether:

> This Government has already taken occasion to inform the Imperial German Government that it cannot admit the adoption of such measures or such a warning of danger to operate in any degree as an abbreviation of the rights of American citizens bound on lawful errands as passengers on merchant ships of belligerent nationality; and that it must hold the German Government to a strict accountability for any infringement of those rights, intentional or incidental. . . . It assumes . . . that the Imperial Government accept, as of course, the rule that the lives the non-combatants, whether they be of neutral citizenship or citizens of one of the nations at war, can not lawfully or rightfully be put in jeopardy by the capture or destruction of an unarmed merchantman. . . .

The objection of the United States to submarine warfare, the note continued, lay precisely in the fact that it was "practically impossible" to observe the elementary principles of international law concerning visit and search. An extraordinary and startling conclusion followed, no less so because it was obvious: "Manifestly submarines cannot be used against merchantment, as the last few weeks have shown, without an inevitable violation of many sacred principles of justice and humanity." The note concluded with finality: "The Imperial German Government will not expect the Government of the United States to omit any word or any act necessary to the performance of its sacred duty of maintaining the rights of the United States and its citizens."[26]

Wilson's stern note had no lack of public support. There was the most convincing evidence that he had satisfied the great mass of American opinion. The *Baltimore Sun* believed that there was "all the blood in the message that a red-blooded nation can ask." The people stood "behind him to a man" said the *Boston Transcript*. On the front page of the *New York Times* for May 13th the note was printed in its entirety with an eight column banner headline.

PRESIDENT TELLS GERMANY WE WILL OMIT NO WORD OR
ACT REQUIRED BY THE SACRED DUTY OF MAINTAINING OUR
RIGHTS, VIOLATED BY SUBMARINE WAR ON MERCHANT SHIPS:
APPEALS TO GERMAN SENSE OF JUSTICE AND HUMANITY

The *Times* editorial was likewise certain that the President "had the united support of the people," while according to the *Chicago Tribune*, he had "voiced the sentiment of the nation." The *New Republic* said that it "reproduced with remarkable skill the mean of American opinion. It represents the picture of a nation seeking by all honorable means to avoid war, but willing to go even to that extreme in defense of principles of law and humanity." Wilson was deeply touched by this support, and after a tumultuous reception in New York on May 17th he expressed once again in a brief address his belief that "the force of America is the force of moral principle, . . . there is nothing else for which she will contend."[27]

The legitimacy of this stand on moral consensus was not recognized by the German Government in its long-awaited reply on May 31st. Before Wilson's demands could be met, it insisted, there must first be agreement "that the reports of the facts which are before the two Governments are complete." The American protest assumed from the start that the *Lusitania* was an ordinary unarmed merchant vessel, whereas, on the contrary, she was an auxiliary cruiser of the British navy, built at Admiralty expense and expressly included in its navy list. All such cruisers had been fitted with guns, and on the *Lusitania* these were mounted under decks and masked. On her last voyage she carried Canadian troops. Her cargo included over five thousand cases of ammunition, thus violating "the clear provisions of American laws which expressly prohibit, and provide punishment for, the carrying of passengers on ships which have explosives on board." All reports confirm that of the submarine commander "that the rapid sinking of the *Lusitania* was primarily due to the explosion of the cargo of munitions caused by the torpedo. Otherwise, in all human probability, the passengers of the *Lusitania* would have been saved." The cruiser rules of visit and search were not observed here because of another fact: British instructions for merchant ships to seek protection behind neutral flags and, when so disguised, to attack German submarines by ramming them. "The Imperial Government holds the facts recited above to be of sufficient importance to recommend them to a careful examination by the American Government."[28]

This reply raised a serious problem for Wilson's moral position. It said in effect that it was inappropriate for him to insist upon the immorality of the submarine's use against the *Lusitania*, because certain facts in this particular case reduced Germany's accountability, not only for any illegality involved but also for the great loss of life which ensued. Indeed, the United States Government was a partial contributory cause of the disaster, and therefore to some extent itself accountable for the loss of its own citizens' lives. Lansing saw the force of this argument immediately and the very next day insisted to both Bryan and Wilson that "a discussion of the facts of specific cases would be premature before the rights asserted in the American note had been admitted." To which Bryan promptly replied: "Suppose. . . . it was Germany's understanding that no Americans were on the vessel and, therefore, none could have been drowned. If that was the fact questioned is there any reason why we should answer 'you must first tell us what you would do in case American citizens were drowned and then we will discuss whether they were drowned or not'? . . . I do not see how we can reasonably refuse to consider a question of fact when it is properly raised."[29]

Certain of these facts could be dealt with more easily than others, thought Bryan. On June 4th a lengthy memorandum arrived from Dudley Field Malone, the Collector of Customs in New York, afterward called the Malone Report, which gave ample evidence for the absence of Canadian troops. Nor had Canadian troops embarked from New York on any previous voyage. Malone also stated that his "neutrality squad," as well as he himself, had inspected the decks of the *Lusitania* one hour before departure and had found "no guns of any character, mounted or unmounted, masked or unmasked," although bases for six inch guns were found riveted to the steel structure and covered with wooden planking.[30] As for the fear of ramming, Bryan agreed with Lansing that it should not be taken seriously. The submarine commander could scarcely have believed that a liner of over 31,000 tons could maneuver fast enough to ram something as small and swift as a submarine. And the use of neutral flags certainly ought not be raised in this case, since there was no doubt at all that the *Lusitania* was flying a belligerent flag when the torpedo was fired.

There were two facts, however, insisted Bryan, which should give the President serious concern. The first of these was that we had not warned our citizens against taking unnecessary risks when precedents for so doing were abundant, Americans had been warned to leave Mexico, for example, "not because they did not have a right to stay there, but because we thought it unwise for them to incur the risks involved in staying. Those who remained were told of the danger in so doing. It seems to me that we cannot well justify a failure to warn American citizens against going into the danger zone on foreign ships—especially ships which, by carrying ammunition, invite extraordinary risks." Do not authorities in time of riot, as a matter of precaution, restrain citizens from the exercise of their rights in order to prevent injuries? By not giving such a warning were we not saying in effect that the ammunition on the *Lusitania*, intended for a belligerent, should be safeguarded in transit by the lives of American citizens? In replying to Germans, moreover, we must "bear in mind that our only concern is with the protection of our people. We have not felt called upon to express an opinion on submarine warfare when other vessels not bearing Americans have been sunk. Whatever views we may have as to the moral character of the means employed by the belligerents, we do not feel it our duty to express opinions merely for the purpose of announcing our views."[31]

The other fact, "the most serious one raised," concerned the ammunition itself. Was our law violated or not? Wilson must have noted especially Bryan's fear of "the moral effect of a position which would make us seem to acquiesce in the carrying of American citizens with ammunition in violation of law."[32] The Malone Report, which arrived the day after Bryan voiced this concern, quoted a 1911 ruling of the Department of Commerce and Labor which allowed the transportation "without restriction" of "small arms ammunition" on passenger ships, since these can be subjected to "rough usage" without risk of explosion. This ruling modified an earlier statute imposing an absolute embargo on the shipment of munitions with passengers. Malone concluded that the ammunition in the *Lusitania's* cargo *"did not contain explosives within the interpretation of our statutes and regulations."*[33] There was obviously here no evidence denying the actual explosion of this ammunition, only an assertion that it did not technically constitute "high explosives" and so could be allowed in strict legality to be shipped along with passengers. At the end of his report Malone attached a summary of the *Lusitania's* complete manifest, including an itemizing of all the legally permitted contraband. None of this satisfied Bryan. The fact that the ammunition could be legally justified simply meant that the 1911 ruling was a very lax interpretation for wartime: "rough usage" could not possibly have envisioned attack by a torpedo. Would the nation absolve its Government from some accountability here?

Bryan apparently was not overconcerned with the issue of armament. Nevertheless, this eventually became a third fact that had to be taken seriously. It was not disposed of by the Malone Report as easily as might appear, because it raised the whole question of the *Lusitania's* wartime status. We already noted Wilson's query to Bryan on April 6th:

> If *some* British merchantmen were known to be armed and the British Government had in fact authorized or advised all merchantmen to arm themselves against submarines, and assuming it to have been impractical for the German commander to ascertain whether the *Falaba* was armed, *was he justified in the circumstances* in acting upon the theory that the British authorization had in effect transformed *all* British merchantmen into public armed vessels and made them liable to attack as such?[34]

Bryan now urged the President on June 3rd to take into account the fact that secret instructions to British merchantmen to ram submarines may have altered the status of the *Lusitania* in regard to submarines, though her general status might have remained that of an unarmed liner. "In other words, if a submarine is to be bound by the rules applicable to merchantmen, then the merchantmen ought also be bound by the rules applicable when merchantmen are attacked by a cruiser."[35] And even Lansing admitted on June 7th that the "only question which might be considered as possible of investigation would be whether or not the *Lusitania* was an auxiliary of the British navy, but this appears to me so manifestly contradicted by the presence of passengers on board and the vessel clearing on its regular trade route, that it offers slender excuse for an inquiry."[36] Yet he himself had secretly made such an inquiry of the Government's legal department shortly after May 10th. Their reply was that British policy had obliterated the distinction between merchantmen and men of war and that Germany had every right to sink the *Lusitania* to prevent a valuable cargo of munitions from going to Germany's enemies.[37] This might possibly explain why he had, in vain, urged Wilson to change the phrase "unarmed merchantman" to "unresisting merchantman" in the first *Lusitania* note, and why he gave as a reason: "The use of the adjective 'unarmed' . . . implied that if *armed* a vessel changed her status and was subject to different treatment. . . ."[38]

Lansing was too good a lawyer not to know that all three of these facts could be legally justified. It could easily be shown that the Government had no strict duty either to warn Americans off belligerent ships, or to prohibit transportation of small arms ammunition on passenger ships, or to question the status of the *Lusitania* even if she were carrying six inch guns. (There was no legal duty in the latter case because, as we saw, guns of such calibre were technically considered to be defensive armament, and the State Department had agreed at the outbreak of the war that this would not make a vessel a warship.)[39] The question, however, was whether these facts could be *morally* justified. Wilson's protest over the *Lusitania* was moral indignation writ large, deliberately intended to voice the consensus of the nation as a whole. But would the people have allowed him to speak as he did if these facts were generally known?

Lansing obviously thought not. We have already noted his opposition to warning Americans after the sinking because this "would be to admit that the Government of the United States failed in its duty," a reason Wilson accepted as "unanswerable," although he conceded that it might have been "just" to have issued such a warning.[40] Now Lansing counseled the President again through Bryan: "I do not think that if all the facts alleged by the German Government in its note were true, that they would be relevant to the real question at issue, which is a question of right. While I fully appreciate the decided advantage it would be to leave open a door of discussion as to the facts in the case, I cannot bring myself to admit that the facts are pertinent and entitled to investigation."[41] As it turned out, both he and Wilson had in mind the fact of the munitions cargo and the fact of armament. Any public acknowledgement that such facts were open to investigation would have at once compromised the whole moral stance of the protest and reduced to ambiguity its appeal to the rights of humanity.

IV

We do not know whether Bryan's telling observations really disturbed Wilson in these early days of June. What is clear, however, is that very soon after the German reply of May 31st the President determined that in his second *Lusitania* note nothing must interfere with his ability to focus upon loss of life by a barbaric weapon. Count von Bernstorff, the German Ambassador, spoke with him on June 2nd and reported to Berlin that "Wilson kept coming back to the point that to him only humanitarian considerations are important. . . . His efforts are directed at a total abolition of the submarine war. . . . In giving up the submarine war, we should base our action on moral grounds, since only by reaching an understanding on moral grounds, and not by weapons, can the war be decided. . . . The American note of reply will probably subordinate all juridical issues and stress only the human."[42] This central point must not be obscured, the President told Bryan: "We cannot afford even to seem to be trying to make it easier for Germany to accede to our demands by turning in similar fashion to England. . . . It would be so evident a case of uneasiness and hedging that I think it would weaken our whole position fatally." And on June 2nd, evidently after the von Bernstorff interview, he noted again: "It is interesting and significant how often the German Foreign Office goes over the same ground in different words, and always misses the essential point involved, that England's violation of neutral rights is different from Germany's violation of the rights of humanity."[43]

Relying on much of Lansing's data, Wilson typed a first draft of his note almost at one sitting on June 3rd, going over it with Bryan and then the whole Cabinet on June 4th. The revisions continued until the 8th, with the final version ready on the 9th. Almost none of Bryan's suggestions were followed, and his total of six letters since June 1st, some very long, went for nothing in the end. It was this Government's duty, Wilson said, "to see to it that the *Lusitania* was not armed for offensive action [the use of "offensive" made it irrelevant whether she carried "defensive" armament], that she was not serving as a transport, that she did not carry cargo prohibited by the statutes of the United States [the nature of the cargo thus became irrelevant], and that, if in fact she was a naval vessel of Great Britain, she should not receive clearance as a merchantman [the fact of clearance thus determining naval status]; and it performed that duty and enforced its statutes with scrupulous vigilance through its regularly constituted officials." Contentions regarding the nature of the cargo and its possible explosion by the torpedo "are irrelevant to the question of the legality of the method used by the German authorities in sinking the vessel." Indeed,

> the sinking of passenger ships involves principles of humanity which throw into the background any special circumstances of detail that may be thought to affect the case. . . . Whatever be the other facts regarding the *Lusitania*, the principal fact is that a great steamer, primarily and chiefly a conveyance for passengers . . . was torpedoed and sunk without so much as a challenge or a warning, and that men, women and children were sent to their death in circumstances unparalleled in modern warfare. . . . The Government of the United States is contending for something much greater than mere rights of property or privileges of commerce. It is contending for nothing less high and sacred than the rights of humanity, which every Government honors itself in respecting and which no Government is justified in resigning on behalf of those under its care and authority. Only her actual resistance to capture or refusal to stop . . . could have afforded the commander of the submarine any justification for so much as putting the lives of those on

board in jeopardy. . . . It is upon this principle of humanity as well as upon the law founded upon this principle that the United States must stand.[44]

Wilson was well aware that this "high ground" of protest involved risk. "I wish with all my heart," he wrote on June 7th, "that I saw a way to carry out the double wish of our people, to maintain a firm front in respect of what we demand of Germany and yet do nothing that might by any possibility involve war."[45] Bryan was convinced that the tone of the note finally committed the nation to a policy that made war not only possible but inevitable. In conscience he could not sign it, and on June 8th, the day before it was dispatched, he resigned. That war did not follow immediately was due only to the fact that both the German Generals and the German Foreign Office agreed that for the present the risk of war was not commensurate with the results to be obtained by a limited U-boat fleet. Another year would pass before the small fleet of thirty submarines would be large enough to inflict damage for the risk once more to be placed in the balance and this time chosen.

Meanwhile in Berlin Chancellor Bethmann-Hollweg, overriding von Tirpitz and the naval staff, secured on August 30th an order from the Kaiser specifically forbidding the destruction of any passenger ships without giving warning or without assuring the safety of passengers and crew. Since German naval commanders considered obedience to these orders impracticable, they suspended all submarine warfare against commerce.[46] For the time being Germany chose to surrender her only weapon on the seas and to give Wilson a diplomatic victory. Yet at this advanced stage of relations all the important decisions had been made as far as the United States was concerned. This country's entry into the war now depended not upon any stand to be taken in the future but upon the entrenched position of the two *Lusitania* notes. When Berlin eventually renewed unrestricted submarine warfare in 1917, this country was forced to declare war. For we had in effect said the last word first.

Talleyrand said of the murder of the Duc d'Enghien that it was worse than a crime, it was a blunder. In the eyes of Americans the sinking of the *Lusitania* was indeed a crime, but it also branded Germany with the moral stigma of a heinous aggressor, capable of defying the laws of God and man by using a lawless weapon unknown to civilized warfare. The spectacle of innocent passengers made victims of the submarine produced an outrage unrelieved by mitigating circumstance of contributory responsibility. Wilson used this outrage, which was a replica of his own, to articulate a moral consensus which he knew he could enforce by the ultimate sanction of war. But for him to do so there had to be no discomfort on the part of the people in locating accountability. There must be no public discussion of warnings or of armament or of cargo; no doubts about the right to apply to this disaster the principles upon which all were agreed. The Malone Report must therefore be kept secret, not even released to the British Court of Inquiry, for it contained too much information about the cargo and about the tenuous legal justification of allowing ammunition on passenger liners. When the British made their initial request, Lansing, now Acting Secretary of State, sent to the Treasury Department for the Report but was told the President had it. He then wrote Wilson, who replied on June 16th that the British would have to be satisfied with sworn statements of customs officers.[47] At this time the President placed the only copy of the full twenty-five page *Lusitania* manifest in a sealed envelope, marked it "Only to be opened by the President of the United States," and deposited it in the Treasury archives.[48]

An even more difficult decision presented itself on June 22nd, when the Austrian Ambassador, Constantin Dumba, sent Lansing information, carefully researched and documented, which proved that several hundred tons of pyroxylin, a type of gun cotton which becomes highly explosive when brought into contact with seawater, had been sent to the *Lusitania* for shipment on its last voyage. (No record of this appeared on the manifest, but the unusual packaging of the pyroxylin corresponded in numbers and weight to the 3,813 forty-pound packages of cheese.) Lansing had all the documentation checked and found it to be accurate. On June 24th Dr. E. W. Ritter von Rettegh, a naturalized American citizen and well-known expert on explosives, who submitted the affidavit on the high-explosive potential of pyroxylin and seawater, was arrested in Cleveland. The initial charge was check offenses, but this was changed on August 2nd to "utterances prejudicial to the peace of the Nation." He was convicted and sentenced to one to three years in prison. The trial was not public and no evidence in it is available. Two witnesses against him were a secret agent of the Treasury Department and a special agent of the Justice Department. The U.S. Attorney-General instructed the Cleveland attorney-general on no account to release any information on Ritter von Rettegh to the press. The file on him and his trial is still classified as secret in the Justice Department archives.[49]

There was also danger at this time that the armament question might become a topic of public discussion. As we have seen, all the evidence after the sinking pointed to the absence of six inch guns, and even if the *Lusitania* had been so armed, such defensive weapons would not have altered her legal status or dispensed with the duty to visit and search. In 1913, however, the *New York Tribune* had carried a story that Cunard officials were acknowledging plans for equipping the liner "with high power naval rifles in conformity with England's new policy of arming passenger boats," and in 1914 the *Lusitania* had been listed under "Armed Merchantmen" in the *British Naval Pocketbook For 1914.*[50] Even though such circumstantial evidence proved nothing when weighed against the Malone Report and the unanimous testimony of passengers, there must nevertheless have been apprehension in Washington that attention might be called to it and the whole question of the *Lusitania's* status opened up to public scrutiny.

Only some such fear as this can explain the overkill reaction to the affidavit of Gustav Stahl. Stahl was German, had worked as a steward on the German lines, and had some clandestine relationship with the German Consulate in New York. He was on the liner only a short time before she sailed, yet he testified that, in helping a friend get his baggage aboard, he had seen concealed guns. Who was going to take such a witness seriously? Yet on June 3rd he was arrested by Secret Service agents, charged with perjury, and kept in prison for three months without trial. When he was finally tried in September he pleaded guilty, received an eighteen month sentence, and soon afterward was deported to Switzerland.[51] There is no way of knowing who was ultimately responsible for this treatment of Stahl, or even for that of Ritter von Rettegh, but it is difficult not to conclude that it originated in White House policy.

We are now in a position to summarize the efforts of President Wilson to control the use of the submarines. When Germany announced in February 1915 that she could no longer follow the cruiser rules of visit and search in submarine attacks upon commerce, Wilson resorted to an established principle of international law by a warning that Germany would be held strictly accountable for any American lives lost on American ships as a result of such illegal attacks. It quickly became clear, however, that, the cruiser rules having been made for surface vessels, no law really existed which could be applied to the submarine in wartime. This led Wilson to conclude, as submarine attacks without warning continued during February, March, and April, that he must resort to another means of control; the United States must exercise its mission to vindicate moral principle by declaring its judgment that such warfare violated the rights of humanity. The occasion for enunciating this popular consensus was American rage and indignation at the heavy loss of life when the *Lusitania* was torpedoed in early May.

In order to give his moral protest the necessary teeth, however, Wilson had to do two things. He had to relate this consensus to the legal basis of his previous warning, which he did by interpreting that warning as having meant all along a guaranty of American safety on belligerent ships. While such an interpretation could not be justified in law, the President's belief (or desire to believe) that it could, led him to forgo any attempt to keep Americans off belligerent ships (thus contributing to their deaths on the *Lusitania*). Secondly, he had to prevent any widespread public discussion of whether the *Lusitania* was armed or carried ammunition, since such facts (even if they might be defended legally), could never be morally justified in the popular mind, either because they gave the submarine commander an excusing cause (fear of superior armament) or because they explained why the ship sank so quickly (exploding ammunition). To prevent this blunting of popular protest, Wilson concealed data on both subjects. In the short run his use of moral consensus was effective: rather than risk war with the United States in 1915, Germany abandoned altogether the use of her new weapon against commerce. But in the long run his stubborn stand on principle in this case brought the two nations into armed conflict in World War I.

V

Power is the greatest crime, said William Faulkner, mitigated only by responsibility. In spite of the complete record, locating moral responsibility in the *Lusitania* sinking is not easy. Although we can state moral principles and conclude that they ought to apply to particular situations, we cannot accurately measure moral justification, especially when we are dealing with the mindsets of people who lived seventy years ago. Let us focus first on the Germans. A key fact here is the legal status of all British merchant ships as a result of that government's policy of arming a great many, including fast ocean liners, and actually listing the latter officially as auxiliary cruisers of the British navy. There were also the very specific Admiralty orders for merchantmen to ram submarines and to fire on them at sight, as well as the standard policy of shipping munitions on passenger liners. All this made it extremely difficult for the Germans to discriminate between a liner like the *Lusitania* and an ordinary cargo ship. Should we expect them to have been more scrupulous than the British in an area where the British themselves made no distinctions?

On the other hand, German orders to submarines to sink all enemy shipping without discrimination clearly disregarded the basic moral principle of proportionality. Some proportion must exist between the intent of an act and its consequences. The risk of an extraordinary loss of innocent lives, a very likely consequence of torpedoing a great passenger liner, was altogether disproportionate to the German aim of destroying British property on the seas. Even granting the fact that under ordinary circumstances the *Lusitania* would not have sunk for hours after a single torpedo, the destruction of property would still not have been worth it. Even without munitions, there would still have been risk to life from possible coal bunker explosion, and it is interesting that Captain Schwieger's log book notes this as the more likely cause of the second explosion. This disregard of the risk was the main point of Wilson's protest, and in making it he was on firm moral ground.

These official policies of England and Germany placed the submarine commander in an almost impossible moral position. We have no way of knowing whether he actually had any scruple before he fired his torpedo (though he admits to one afterward and to its preventing him from firing a second time). We do know, however, that he could not have intended the great loss of life. The startled surprise in his log book at the rapid sinking indicates how well aware he was that a single torpedo would not have sunk ships even half the size before passengers and crew had time to launch their lifeboats: another explosion had to intervene to destroy the ship so quickly. In any event, given the policies of the two governments, he was hardly in a position to make an informed moral judgment as to whether or not to fire on the ship before him. Too many factors tended to inhibit such a judgment, and his choice to attack the *Lusitania* became, like so much else in the affair, an ambiguous one from the viewpoint of moral responsibility.

The accountability of the American government is even more difficult to assess. Surely there was neglect of its primary "role-responsibility" to protect the lives of its citizens, at least to the extent of warning them not to travel on belligerent ships. Had there been no Americans on the *Lusitania* there might still have been waves of indignation against Germany, but such indignation would not have resulted in "strict accountability" notes, any more than had the invasion of Belgium nine months earlier. As we saw, Wilson grudgingly admitted that he may have failed in his responsibility to warn, but he insisted to Bryan that it was too late to remedy such failure once the *Lusitania* was sunk. This judgment was unfortunate, since public knowledge of the failure would have served to diffuse responsibility for the heavy loss of life and thereby shortcircuit much of the moral indignation. As it was, full accountability for the disaster fell upon Germany, unmitigated by public awareness that a warning from Washington could have saved many American lives.

On the other hand, the torpedoing of a passenger liner without warning was unquestionably a barbaric deed, and it was right for the United States to distinguish here between property rights and human rights, and to press for the defense of the latter in the midst of the chaos of war. If there was a public consensus in America that the submarine was an inhumane weapon, then Wilson was justified in voicing that consensus and in taking action to limit the submarine's use or to exclude it altogether from combat. Yet once again, this prerogative of the United States was to protest, not to go to war. The threat of war, which backed up the protest, was due not to the barbaric character of the sinking but to the fact that American lives were lost, and this in turn was due to Wilson's failure to warn Americans off belligerent ships. Taken by itself, however, the "high ground" of the *Lusitania* notes was a legitimate expression of the nation's belief that in wartime innocent lives ought not to be needlessly destroyed.

The paradox is that this moral consensus was so strong because it was so completely uninformed. The concealment responsible for this was neither cowardly nor petty. If pressed on the point, Wilson would probably have said that what he did was justified in order to keep clear his mandate from the country to protest the violation of human rights. Conventional law was impotent to control the submarine, but moral consensus might, and the tragedy of May 7th was the perfect occasion to exert the required pressure on Germany. The need to keep this pressure high was justification enough to conceal those facts of contributory negligence urged upon him by a sometimes frantic Bryan. Theoretically such a line of reasoning might be valid, but concretely a much harder test would have to be applied, since the moral protest of the *Lusitania* notes was backed up by the threat of war, by the demand for a "strict accountability." In the area of morals as in that of law, there is no such thing as principles "in the air." In order for the United States to take on responsibility actually to intervene in the war, there would have to have been a much more searching evaluation than there was of all the relevant facts of the sinking.

Such an investigation would, of course, have disclosed how ambiguous an event the disaster really was, how incapable of bearing, from the viewpoint of either law or morality, all the weight that was placed upon it. Ambiguity of this kind was a very difficult thing for Wilson to support. "I feel keenly the force of your counter judgment," he wrote Bryan, "and I cannot claim that I feel cock sure of the rightness of my own conclusion." And just before the Secretary's resignation he admitted that "it is with deep misgivings that I turn from what you press upon me."[52] We should be inclined to say in retrospect today that for Wilson to have risked involving the country in a major war over the *Lusitania* disaster was a blunder of major proportions. But we make that judgment with seventy years of hindsight. Looking back over the time we can easily be cool in dealing with an event that aroused only outrage, well informed and objective on questions which then had to be settled on the basis of conflicting and impassioned opinion. Many years before the war Wilson sensed this danger of hindsight and we may well conclude with this plea of his for understanding:

> It is easy to be wise out of books, but it is infinitely more difficult to be wise in the midst of affairs. The man who sits in the calmness and stillness of a study and cavils at a man who is in the midst of the infinitely various and difficult affairs of the actual arena of public matters should be very careful to revise his judgments before he utters them and to realize the difficulties before he condemns the man.[53]

6

Natural Law:
A Case Study

The case I wish to study in this chapter is that of the public moral teaching of a particular religious group, the Roman Catholic church. What I will focus on is this church's teaching in the public sphere concerning matters of universal morality proposed as obligatory on all, Catholic and non-Catholic alike. The warrant presented for such teaching is not the Catholic church's religious faith, but rather a universal natural moral law, which is in principle available to all and open to general scrutiny. This concept of a "natural law" has in recent years occasioned considerable curiosity and not a little confusion in the popular mind. One source of the confusion is the obvious need to distinguish physical natural law, or law as uniformity (like gravity, which cannot be disputed nor freely transgressed), from moral natural law, or law as norm of conduct. Another source is the fact that medieval and modern conceptions of this moral natural law can really constitute different doctrines altogether, and it is not always clear which particular doctrine is under discussion. There is very little in common, for example, between the ideas of thirteenth century scholastic thinkers on the subject and the ideas that energized the American and French revolutions or that now challenge us in the writings of twentieth-century philosophers.

But in spite of these confusions, public interest and curiosity continue, due in large part, I think, to the constant reliance on this concept of natural law in the official public documents of the Roman Catholic church. Such reliance has in fact been the single most important element in traditional Catholic understanding of morality, and has been the chief argument for the church's claim to teach a morality that is universal and applicable to all. Hence in order to see how this church understands the common good in matters of public morality, we shall have to examine first its natural law tradition. What precisely are its origins? How has this tradition been applied over the years to social and sexual morality? What is its status today? This tradition's point of departure has always been the medieval concept of natural law, and so it is there that we must begin. Little attention has ever been given in official teaching to any other approach to natural law. This medieval tradition, however, was itself a synthesis. The Schoolmen, and especially Thomas Aquinas, wove together two main threads from the classical authors, the idea that natural law represented a higher ideal of justice in society, and the very different idea that it represented an animal instinct and a physical structure. Let us examine this synthesis more closely.

I

Cicero wrote eloquently of natural law as "right reason in agreement with nature, of universal application, unchanging and everlasting. . . . There will not be a different law at Rome and at Athens, a different law now and in the future, but one eternal and unchangeable law for all nations and for all times."[1] This ideal goes back to the *Antigone* of Sophocles, the notion of an eternal and immutable justice, which human authority ought to express but frequently does not. Natural law in the very different sense of animal instinct seems to have begun with the definition of Ulpian, a third-century lawyer, whose writings constituted almost a third of the *Code of Justinian*. "Natural law indeed is not peculiar to the human race, but belongs to all animals."[2] This outlook tends to focus upon the physical and biological structure of acts as the source of morality, especially sexual morality, and to shift perspective away from the moral questions with less "physicality," such as economic justice and the norms for judging the rectitude of civil law.

Aquinas managed to combine these two threads. He understood natural law as a call to human beings to participate intellectually and actively in the eternal law, that rational ordering of the universe by a provident God. "Among all others, the rational creature is subject to divine providence in a more excellent way, insofar as it itself partakes of a share of providence by being provident both for itself and others. Therefore it has a share of the eternal reason, whereby it has a natural inclination to its proper act and end; and this participation of the eternal law in the rational creature is called the 'natural law'."[3] More concretely, natural law is that inclination in all humans to know and seek what is good for themselves, and to live in society according to this knowledge through the enactment of just civil law. But, precisely as animals, humans also have all those inclinations which animals have generally, and so these too must pertain to natural law. Unlike animals, however, humans consciously reflect upon this second set of inclinations and subject them to rational control.[4] They are thus not to be identified with natural law (though they might be called a law of nature); natural law is rather their recognition and the reasoned insight into how they should be followed in a given case.

This medieval effort was so valuable at the time because it opened up the possibility of giving a rational explanation for moral imperatives, an ethic based upon human existence as experienced, independently of any divine revelation. Aquinas wanted to establish some rational standard by which social and political institutions could be judged, a court of appeal, as it were, for the rejection of unjust laws. His natural law theory served importantly as a safeguard against government abuses, against the tyrannical assertion that human law was the pure command of the ruler. It was therefore a theory of what makes laws laws, what gives them obligatory force. Only in a most secondary sense was its function to be that of positive civil law, namely to give explicit directives, since those directives which Aquinas believed were known clearly to everyone are of such a general character as seldom to give specific guidance regarding concrete decisions. Indeed, his first formal principle of natural law (good is to be done and evil avoided), as well as its primary areas of material specification (the inclination to preservation of life, generation and education of offspring, organization of society), were meant to focus less upon their content than upon the obligatory force somehow inherent in them, which is indeed universal and immutable: something should be done to preserve life, to organize the family, and to stabilize society. In the concrete this "somehow" and this "something" had to be derived from experience and enquiry by way of conclusion from these general principles. "What pertains to moral science," said Aquinas, "is known mostly through experience."[5]

From such an emphasis upon experience it followed that exceptions, disagreements, and the danger of making mistakes increase the more detailed these conclusions become. Whatever natural law may in fact demand in a concrete circumstance, therefore, need not be either rigidly applied universally nor clearly recognized by everyone who acts rationally.[6] For once one descends from first principles, the task of drawing detailed conclusions is simply too difficult, not only because of the innate weakness of human intelligence, but also because of the clouding of our self-knowledge by habit, prejudice, ignorance, and passion. Prudent estimates are the most we can expect in the majority of situations. Yet as responsible persons we must use what knowledge we have to shape our lives as best we can. This effort is all the more difficult insofar as we are continually confronted in the modern world with totally new situations. The human species has been developing over many centuries, and its maturity is evident today. We have only to think of the sophisticated dilemmas we must now face in bioethics to be aware of our constant need to draw from general principles ever new conclusions, unknown and unsought by former generations. Earlier conclusions may even need to be modified in these changed circumstances, or discarded altogether as having no further application. Aquinas easily allowed for such change in conclusions from general principle, since he clearly believed that our knowledge of natural law can change and that human nature itself is not wholly immutable, something his interpreters have only recently been willing to admit.[7]

What then is the value and function of this medieval theory of natural law? On the social level, the most we can say is that it provides us with a criterion, a rational structure, whereby good laws may be seen to be good laws. As one authority has put it, "It represents a pattern of law as law, discoverable, as patterns are, by those who enquire diligently; it might even be described as the special logic of law, as ever present and necessary to law as logic is to argument. . . . And as we may justify or invalidate an argument by appeal to logic, so we may justify or invalidate the laws of men by appeal to the natural law."[8] On a more individual level, the "nature" metaphor expresses that inner drive we all feel toward authentic personhood and self-realization, a tendency rather than a code, "dy-namically inviting possibility, a concrete project to be carried out in the midst of a concrete situation."[9] On both these levels moral striving is a constant, but its constancy is not that of a law in a legalistic or static sense, but that of an inbuilt direct-edness toward one's end. This dynamic bent in human per-sons, according to Aquinas, is perceived by practical reason on the conscious level in the form of moral imperatives, which in turn become the actions constituting the concrete conclu-sions of natural law.[10]

II

The primary purpose for the development of this medieval theory of natural law was, as I said, to establish some order in the political and social institutions of Western Europe. Those who suffered from predatory overlords had to be given guid-ance and protection, and the Catholic church of the time tried to do both. Rarely, however, was natural law ever mentioned in the official teaching of church documents. Rarer still were attempts to ground in natural law theory those centuries-old prohibitions agains fornication, divorce, birth control, or abor-tion. All these prohibitions were presumed to be clearly pres-ent in the Sacred Scripture and were so presented to the faithful long before the medieval synthesis.[11] Only in the last century, when Leo XIII chose Thomistic philosophy as the model for Catholic schools, did Catholic moralists begin seriously to high-light natural law theory as the warrant for specific moral teaching.

Leo himself was indeed very close to Aquinas' original con-cerns when he treated questions of social morality from a nat-ural law perspective: the right to private property and a just wage, the right of workers to organize, etc. Pius XI followed this same general approach when commenting on national socialism in Germany, for example, as well as on the rights of parents to educate children, and on labor-management rela-tions in *Quadragesimo Anno*. The public treaties of Pius XII did the same in seeking to ground upon a natural moral order the great political, social, and international issues of his long pon-tificate. In *Pacem in Terris* John XXIII could address his discus-sion of rights to all persons of good will, not just to Christians, because he emphasized that freedom and intelligence are images of the divine in all men and women, and that human reason is therefore capable of discovering these demands of human dignity placed in creatures by the Creator.

In none of these papal documents, however, was there any effort to deduce detailed conclusions from the first principles of natural law. The emphasis was consistently upon a very general recognition of the rights of persons through appeal to legal philosophy, anthropology, and data from the social sciences, an approach accepted by many who would never subscribe to the scholastic understanding of natural law. The popes' claim was that all reasonable people should be able to discern a human right to minimum levels of food, clothing, and shelter, the values of work and family, the binding nature of contracts, as well as the need for both freedom and interdependence. At the same time there was also a claim, quite consistent with natural law theory, that Christian faith can make a significant contribution to social morality, because in fact these moral insights of reasonable people correspond with traditional Christian values and teaching. All these documents speak of "reason enlightened by revelation." Coherence between these two claims has indeed been one of the basic methodological principles of the popes' pronouncements on social morality.[12]

The Roman Catholic church's competence to interpret natural moral law regarding social justice thus appears presented as clearly a negative competence: reason cannot contradict any of the ethical principles of fundamental Christian doctrine. The task of the church is to shape certain patterns of thinking which follow from this revealed doctrine and then to use these patterns as a check upon movements in society with potential to damage human life. Such "critical negativity," to use Edward Schillebeeckx's phrase, is a positive power exercising constant pressure to bring about what is most desirable for society, not by explicit detailed formulations, but by negative knowledge. For in strictly human and secular concerns the church has as little positive idea as nonbelievers of what is most worthy of the human person. Popes must consider various alternatives, keeping in mind, as they search, human values already realized in history. If they protest certain public situations or goals, they do so in the name of values still sought by humankind and contained negatively in Christian revelation, that is, in the experience of what is unworthy of human dignity.

This does not mean, of course, that the church cannot condemn a very specific social evil as an affront to the human person. In the agrarian world of the Middle Ages, for example, the prevailing forms of usury were clearly harmful. Everyone agrees now that it was wise for the church to prohibit interest on loans at that time, in a culture where all loans were agricultural and where the exploited were always poor peasants dependent upon changing weather. It was a mistake, however, to have been seduced by circumstances of a particular time and place into thinking and declaring an expedient economic policy to be an immutable truth of Christian morals, simply because it was a conclusion reasonable persons could at that time deduce from the first principles of natural law. For centuries the church proclaimed this prohibition as unchangeable doctrine. As Europe moved into the new commercial civilization of the Renaissance, the force of church authority thus prevented good loans as well as bad. Aquinas' insistence on the time-bound nature of all conclusions from natural law principles could have avoided this. "Practical reason," he had said, "being concerned with human conduct, has to do with the contingent. And so, though there is a certain necessity about its general principles, the further it descends into detail, the more it may encounter exceptions. . . . In the practical order there is not the same truth or practical rightness for everybody, as far as detail is concerned, but only in general principles. . . . "[13]

In economic and social matters the church has never made the usury mistake again. When it has appealed to natural law in these areas it has been careful not to descend into this kind of detail, and it has also tended to understand "natural" in more general terms, as that which belongs to the basic structures of human life recognized by all rational persons. Since the appearance of that very important document of Vatican II, *Gaudium et Spes, the Pastoral Constitution on the Church in the Modern World*, the church's epistemological claim in regard to natural law seems to have become more modest still, more cautious and more nuanced. Roman Catholicism now recognizes more readily the intellectual and cultural pluralism which exists in modern society, and no longer claims privileged insight into concrete conclusions about social obligation, unless these are explicitly related to Christian revelation. Recent documents do not hide the fact that they are proceeding on the basis of non-universal forms of moral reasoning, and whatever certitudes they proclaim have a much more distinctly Christian basis. These documents more easily accept the inevitability of conflict on the philosophical level, as well as on the level of politics and social life, and are content with conclusions on these levels which are ambiguous, partial, and incomplete.[14]

III

This recent approach to natural law in dealing with social morality contrasts strongly with the approach in documents dealing with sexual morality. In the social area, as we saw, the Roman Catholic church has claimed a negative competence to reject ethical positions that contradict statements in revelation about human life. It has also claimed a positive competence to propose moral norms already embraced by the world community and in keeping with its aspirations for justice. But church authority has avoided specifying these norms in detail. It has advocated a just wage for workers, for example, as something in accord with natural law, but it has not used its teaching authority to state what such a wage should be in the concrete (other than that it should provide adequately for the needs of the worker and his family), since circumstances of time and place would introduce serious disagreements and elicit very diverse opinions. This does not mean that the church does not have the authority, if it so wishes, to propose very detailed norms for social morality which are established neither through revelation nor through common human consciousness. But then it would clearly be in the area of contingent human knowledge. Before it did this, dialogue with the larger human community would be absolutely essential for credibility, and any claim that the norms in question were grounded in natural law would have to be supported by serious reasons and argument.

Yet in the area of sexual morality papal documents have consistently proposed just such detailed norms, and have consistently claimed that these norms are to be found in the natural law. Indeed, natural law theory seems to have been viewed over the last century as a refuge against the changing sexual mores of a secular world, a bastion within which moral precepts could be taught with certitude and any violations condemned by absolute prohibition. In *Humanae Vitae*, to take the latest and clearest example, Paul VI was not simply content to reaffirm as a fundamental principle the inseparable unity between love and fecundity in human sexuality, an ideal which would find broad acceptance in the human community. The whole point of the encyclical was rather that this principle must apply to each individual sexual act in marriage: every marriage act must remain open to the transmission of life; there is an inseparable link between its procreative and unitive meanings. While it is permissible directly to contravene this imperative by systematic abstinence during the fertile periods, any artificial contraceptive procedures are intrinsically evil.[15] Pope Paul made no attempt to support this central conclusion from Scripture, nor did he make much of an argument from tradition, citing references to documents going no further back than the last century. He noted that the teaching has been constantly proposed by tradition, but this obviously argued not for its truth but for its longevity. Its truth and certitude, he insisted, come from its firm grounding in the natural moral law.

Why this insistence on such clarity of detail in the natural law regarding sexual morality? The reason is that Catholic moralists of the past, when dealing with sexual matters, opted for a biological concept of nature in the rigid mode of Ulpian, which, as I noted earlier, represented one strand only of the natural law tradition incorporated into the medieval synthesis. They also committed themselves to an obsolete biology, by continuing to attribute a meaning to all sexual acts on the basis of what is now known to happen with relative rarity. This approach is clearly out of touch with much contemporary theological thought, as well as with the whole thrust of the *Pastoral Constitution on the Church in the Modern World*, which sees the human person, not the operations of some isolated human organ, as the fundamental moral criterion for human actions.[16] In other words, biological fertility has to get its moral meaning from its ordination toward those goods which define the total institution of marriage. Pope Paul did not deny that purposes other than biological finality are involved in marital sexuality (a clear advance over Ulpian and the medievalists), but these can be tolerated, he said, only as long as the "nature of the act" is respected (a regression from Vatican II's emphasis on the "nature of the person").[17]

Such an understanding of natural law as identical with natural physical processes is obviously more applicable to sexual than to social matters, and this explains the ease with which the Catholic church has been able to descend into such detail when speaking of sex. But the consequences can be embarrassing, as *Humanae Vitae* proved, for nowhere in the encyclical was the central conclusion shown as following reasonably from a widely accepted general moral principle. The conclusion was simply asserted without supporting argument. This would, of course, be understandable in a document explaining the Catholic church's understanding of divine revelation. But since neither revelation nor infallibility were involved here, the degree of authority behind the teaching remained unjustified, and the responsibility to supply reasons correspondingly more urgent. This was all the more imperative because the conclusion was supposed to derive exclusively from natural law, whose obligatory force is constituted precisely by human reasoning. Not to supply a reasoned argument was therefore to raise the suspicion that none exists. Simply to *declare* that artificial contraception is intrinsically evil was to use authority to deprive natural law in this case of its whole epistemological base and to turn it into a purely juridical concept.[18] It was also to confuse the teaching office of the church with its governing office, since the encyclical's authoritative teaching on natural law inevitably assumed a purely disciplinary connotation that concerned Catholics alone.

The generally strong negative reaction to *Humanae Vitae* as contrary to the lived experience of both Catholics and persons of other faiths raises a host of ecclesiological problems regarding the exercise of the Catholic church's noninfallible teaching authority. How precisely ought this teaching deal with issues of natural law so as to function in more than a juridical way? Is the pope's particular teaching office to be identified with its monarchical expression? Pope Paul appealed to "the light of the Holy Spirit" to substantiate his position on contraception. But does such an appeal imply a power somehow to achieve outside the human process a truth which is in principle accessible to all reasonable persons? Does moral persuasiveness require identifying the various processes within which the Spirit is presumed to be operating? Does it also require a broad consultation at all levels of the church's life, and a listening to this collaborative effort before putting full papal authority behind the assertion that a highly disputed concrete moral norm enjoys the status of a natural law?[19]

Once again, however, as in the case of social morality, the issue is not whether the Roman Catholic Church should propose moral norms in the public sphere. It should. But when these are established neither through its understanding of revelation nor through a general consensus of the human community, then prior dialogue with this community is essential for credibility, and the norms themselves should be proposed only to the extent that valid reasons can be found to ground them in natural law. The more concrete and detailed these norms are, the more imperative this mode of procedure becomes. This is the way for the church to be truly prophetic, as it surely was in the great social encyclicals of the present century. This is how it can truly fulfill a mission to be a moral conscience for the world. Nor should it hesitate to use natural law as a vehicle for its pedagogy, as long as it is faithful to the full range of its own natural law tradition. For that tradition is based not on commands and prohibitions so much as upon human potentiality and rational discussion, and as such it offers a genuine framework for universal public morality.

In chapter one I said that, at least in the United States, no religious body can presume that a message to the wider community beyond its own membership will be exempt from public scrutiny. Pronouncements of the Roman Catholic church, especially when related to a natural law argument, will immediately engage the membership of other churches as well as secular society generally, even if in a given instance these pronouncements are aimed neither at government nor at the political process. Once they have thus entered the public sphere it will be incumbent upon church leadership to use reasoned argument that is accessible to all, believer and unbeliever alike, since the public authority of the pronouncement will inevitably be proportionate to the persuasiveness of the argument. As we saw in this chapter, Catholic teachings on social and sexual morality met with such different receptions precisely because of the very different methodologies used in each. The responsive chord struck by the social teaching came from its recognition of the intellectual and cultural pluralism of modern society, and of the need to establish some coherence between traditional Christian values and the moral aspirations of reasonable people. The teaching on sexual morality, however, was perceived as too narrowly sectarian, too dependent on church authority and too rigidly based upon a biological understanding of human nature, none of which corresponded with the lived experience of most morally responsible adults. The result was that, in this case, credibility with society as a whole was lost, as was the persuasiveness of the morality taught.

Notes

Preface

1. William F. May, *Ideas, Faiths and Feelings* (New York: Oxford University Press, 1983), 147-86.

2. For overviews of this development see Harold J. Berman, *The Interaction of Law and Religion* (Nashville: Abingdon Press, 1974); "Religion and Law," Symposium in the July 1978 issue of *Hastings Law Journal*; Jay Mechling (ed.), *Church, State and Public Policy* (Washington: American Enterprise Institute, 1978); Lynn R. Buzzard (ed.), *Freedom and Faith*, (Westchester, Illinois: Crossway Books, 1982).

3. See especially *The Challenge of Peace: God's Promise and Our Response*, the Pastoral Letter of the U.S. Catholic Bishops on War and Peace (Washington: National Catholic News Conference, 1983). Among the growing literature, see also Michael Walzer, *Just and Unjust Wars* (New York: Basic Books, 1977); Francis X. Winters and Harold P. Ford (eds.), *Ethics and Nuclear Strategy* (New York: Orbis Books, 1977); David Hollenbach, *Nuclear Ethics: A Christian Moral Argument* (New York: Paulist Press, 1983).

4. Christopher F. Mooney, *Inequality and the American Conscience* (New York: Paulist Press, 1982).

5. The debate continues on the various sets of conflicting data now available on this disaster from the governments of the United States, Russia, and Japan, all of whom are still keeping crucial data secret. See Alexander Dallin, *Black Box: KAL 007 and the Superpowers* (Berkeley: University of California Press, 1985). After proceeding methodologically through all the possible explanations for the deviation from course of Flight 007 that brought it over Soviet territory, Dallin concludes that intentionality, not accident, is the most likely one. This is also the conclusion of Oliver Clubb, *KAL Flight 007: The Hidden Story* (Sag Harbor, N.Y.: Permanent Press, 1985). The accident theory is argued at length by Murray Sayle, "KE 007, A Conspiracy of Circumstance," *The New York Review of Books*, April 25, 1985, 44-54, and challenged at length by David E. Pearson, "The Fate of KE 007: An Exchange," *The New York Review of Books*, September 26, 1985, 47-51.

6. The original version of chapter two appeared in volume 12 and chapter four will eventually appear in volume 18 of the *Proceedings* of Villanova University's Theology Institute; original versions of chapter three appeared in the Summer 1983 issue of the *Journal of Law and Religion*; of chapter five in the September 1976 issue of *Thought*; of chapter six in the May 1980 issue of *Concilium*.

Chapter 1

1. Peter L. Berger, *The Sacred Canopy* (New York: Doubleday, 1967), 107.

2. See on this phenomenon Jeffrey K. Hadden, "Religion and the Construction of Social Problems," in Jeffrey K. Hadden and Theodore E. Long (eds.), *Religion and Religiosity in America* (New York: Crossroad, 1983), 17-30.

3. Robert N. Bellah *et al.*, *Habits of the Heart* (Berkeley: University of California Press, 1985), 219.

4. Martin E. Marty, *The Public Church* (New York: Crossroad, 1981).

5. See "Theology and Philosophy in Public," a symposium edited by David Hollenbach, *Theological Studies* 40 (1979): 700-15.

6. John A. Coleman, *An American Strategic Theology* (New York: Paulist Press, 1982), 228-29.

7. See Wilfred Caron, Dierdre Dessingue, and John Liekweg, "Government Restraint on Political Activities of Religious Bodies," in Dean M. Kelly (ed.), *Government Intervention in Religious Affairs* (New York: Pilgrim Press, 1982), 151-64. In 1970 the Supreme Court spoke of such activities of churches precisely as their right: "Adherents of particular faiths and individual churches frequently take strong positions on public issues including . . . vigorous advocacy of legal or constitutional positions. Of course, churches as much as secular bodies and private citizens have that right." *Walz* v. *Tax Commission*, 397 U.S. 664, 670 (1970).

8. Christopher F. Mooney, *Religion and the American Dream* (Philadelphia: Westminster Press, 1977). Anyone who writes on this subject must rely upon the analyses of the phenomenon made by sociologist Robert N. Bellah, most notably in *The Broken Covenant* (New York: Seabury Press, 1975).

9. See John A. Coleman, "The Christian as Citizen," *Commonweal*, September 9, 1983, 457-62.

10. Bellah *et al.*, *op. cit.*, give an extended and nuanced analysis of the power of individualism in American life, especially its capacity to impoverish both public and private life, and so to dominate our language that even speaking about communal commitments can take place only with great difficulty.

11. Ibid., 253-54, citing Theodore Draper, "Hume and Madison: The Secrets of *Federalist Paper* No. 10," *Encounter* 58 (1982): 47.

12. See the extended argument of J. G. A. Pocock, *The Machiavellian Moment* (Princeton: Princeton University Press, 1975), especially Chapter 15, "The Americanization of Virtue," 506-52. Pocock defines (p. 546) the "Machiavellian moment" as "the confrontation of virtue with corruption."

13. See Gary Wills, *Explaining America: The Federalist* (New York: Doubleday & Company, 1981).

14. See John Patrick Diggins, *The Lost Soul of American Politics* (New York: Basic Books, 1984), *passim*.

15. Alexis de Tocqueville, *Democracy in America*, trans. George Lawrence, ed. J. P. Mayer (New York: Doubleday Anchor Books, 1969), 506. I am indebted to the analysis of this individualism in America given by Bellah *et al.* in *Habits of the Heart*, along with their exposition throughout of de Tocqueville's thought.

16. de Tocqueville, *op. cit.*, 527.

17. Bellah *et al.*, *op. cit.*, 250-51.

18. de Tocqueville, *op. cit.*, 287.

19. Bellah *et al.*, 37-38. These authors point out (p. 312) that "habits of the heart" is undoubtedly a reference to the meaning of the word in the Old and New Testaments, where "heart" involves intellect, will, desires, and feelings, and also means "the law written in the heart" of Romans 2:15.

20. de Tocqueville, *op. cit.*, 292.

21. Ibid., 448, 529.

22. Ibid., 529.

23. Richard Reeves, *American Journey* (New York: Simon and Schuster, 1983), 205.

24. This point has been elaborated at some length by Richard John Neuhaus in *The Naked Public Square* (Grand Rapids: Eerdmans, 1984).

25. Bellah *et al.*, *op. cit.*, 232-37, 243-49, give an enlightening analysis of these privatizing religious movements. One point they make (p. 246) is that the mystical religious consciousness of the 1960s, in spite of its individualism, made a contribution to society by sensitizing the nation to issues such as ecology, peace, feminism, and opposition to nuclear weapons.

26. Kennedy addressed this issue on September 12, 1960, when he spoke in Texas to the Greater Houston Ministerial Association. See Theodore H. White, *The Making of the President* (New York: Atheneum, 1961), 591-92.

27. See Ronald B. Flowers, "President Jimmy Carter, Evangelism, Church-State Relations, and Civil Religion," *Journal of Church and State* 25 (1983): 113-32.

28. See "Anatomy of a Landslide," *Time*, November 17, 1980, 31-35;

Everett C. Ladd, "The Brittle Mandate: Electoral Dealignment and the 1980 Presidential Election," *Political Science Quarterly* 96 (1981): 1-25.

29. See, for example, the critique by John Murray Cuddihy in *No Offense: Civil Religion and Protestant Taste* (New York: Seabury, 1978).

30. In *After Virtue* (Notre Dame: University of Notre Dame Press, 1981), Alasdair MacIntyre argues that the moral health of a society demands that all its citizens hold the same certainty and consensus on moral matters. I cannot agree with this judgment, because American society as a whole, in spite of its diversity of opinions on public morality, shares considerable agreement on the importance of the moral virtues in public life as well as considerable admiration for the persons who practice them.

31. In 1985 Geraldine Ferraro reiterated the position she stated during the campaign: "Personal religious convictions have no place in political campaigns or in dictating public policy. I have always felt that the spiritual beliefs of elected representatives are between them and their God, not their government." See *Ferraro: My Story* (New York: Bantam Books, 1985), 211. See also Robert McAfee Brown's perceptive commentary on the reaction of Democrats to the religion issue in "Religion and Politics: Fireworks in a Fog," *The Christian Century*, October 24, 1984, 973-74.

32. The position of the Roman Catholic Church on the morality of abortion is frequently misstated on two points: first, that it is derived from religious faith and not from moral reasoning; second, that it is based on the fact that the fetus is known to be a human person from the moment of conception. The church's position is, on the contrary, like its positions on racism, nuclear warfare, and capital punishment, based on moral argument, whose cogency can and ought to be debated in the public sphere. The position has been stated at some length in an authoritative document of the Sacred Congregation for the Doctrine of the Faith, *Declaration on Abortion* (Washington, D. C.: U.S. Catholic Conference, 1975). In its briefest formulation the argument says that, since there is no way, scientific or otherwise, to ascertain at what point exactly the human fetus becomes a human person (or, in more traditional religious language, when the human soul becomes present in the human body), abortion at any point after conception may in fact be taking the life of an innocent human person; but to risk actually doing such a thing can never be morally justified for any reason in any circumstances; therefore in practice the human fetus must always be treated as if it were in fact a human person at every moment of its existence.

Obviously public debate on this mode of reasoning will center on whether or not, in the first few weeks of pregnancy (when doubts about the existence of a truly human person are higher), there could ever be a justifiable reason in certain circumstances for directly terminating fetal life. Minimally, of course, the human embryo that in fact is not yet a human person is nonetheless nascent human life, and a persuasive argument can be made that such nascent human life should be given the same protection at all stages of its development. We should note also that up to and including the early part of the present century, official Catholic teaching was much more open in acknowledging the force of doubts regarding human personhood in very early pregnancy than it is today. On this last point see Joseph F. Donceel, "Catholic Politicians and Abortion," *America*, February 2, 1985, 81-83.

33. See Mario M. Cuomo, "Religious Belief and Public Morality: A Catholic Governor's Perspective," address delivered at the University of Notre Dame, September 13, 1984, printed in full in *The New York Review of Books*, October 25, 1985, 32-37.

34. A Roman Catholic perspective on this involvement of churches in public policy has been helpfully stated in an address by Joseph Cardinal Bernardin, "The Role of the Religious Leader in the Development of Public Policy," *The Journal of Law and Religion* 2 (1985): 369-79.

35. Another surprise for those who opposed a role for religion in politics was the Rev. Jesse Jackson, who was perhaps the most interesting person in the 1984 Presidential campaign. As heir to Martin Luther King's mantle as major black national leader, his candidacy for the Democratic nomination was clearly motivated by religious as well as political convictions. He freely used religious language and the rhetoric of the black preacher to appeal to his audiences on moral grounds, and to win a hearing for the underprivileged and the disenfranchised. While his political style was unacceptable to mainstream Americans as well as to his party's leaders, he nevertheless succeeded in rallying black voters to a sense of self reliance and in focusing the national spotlight for a time upon such uncomfortable issues as affirmative action, equal opportunity, housing, job training, and urban poverty. In the end he accomplished what no one else had: he reminded people on the bottom and at the margins of society that they had potential at the polls to produce their own leadership.

36. See Philip Rieff, *The Triumph of the Therapeutic* (New York: Harper & Row, 1966); Bellah *et al., op. cit.,* 47ff.

Chapter 2

1. Winfred E. Garrison, "Characteristics of American Organized Religion," *Annals of the American Academy of Political and Social Sciences* 256 (1948):17. Quoted by Sidney E. Mead, *The Lively Experiment: The Shaping of Christianity in America* (New York: Harper and Row, 1963), 192.

2. This observation has been made by a number of authors; for example, Sidney E. Mead, "The Fact of Pluralism and the Persistence of Sectarianism," in Elwyn A. Smith (ed.), *The Religion of the Republic* (Philadelphia: Fortress Press, 1971), 258-59; Loren P. Beth, *The American Theory of Church and State* (Gainesville: University of Florida Press, 1958), 141-42.

3. See Mead, *Lively Experiment*, 5-15; 24-27.

4. Perry G. E. Miller, "The Contribution of the Protestant Churches to Religious Liberty in Colonial America," *Church History* 4 (1935): 57-66. Quoted by Mead, *Lively Experiment*, 19, who notes as another authority for this view Anson Phelps Stokes' three volume *Church and State in the United States*.

5. Saul K. Padover (ed.), *The Complete Jefferson* (New York: Duell, Sloan and Pearce, 1943), 676.

6. Ibid., 538.

7. See the development in Mead, *Lively Experiment*, 60-66.

8. See Richard E. Morgan, *The Politics of Religious Conflict* (New York: Pegasus, 1968), 20-22. Mead has also made this point in "The Fact of Pluralism . . . ," 249-261, as well as Winthrop Hudson, *American Protestantism* (Chicago: University of Chicago Press, 1961), *passim*. The Episcopal Church, which has always had difficulty with the anti-authoritarian stance of other Protestant churches, is an obvious exception to this generalization.

9. Milton Himmelfarb, "Secular Society? A Jewish Perspective," in William G. McLaughlin and Robert N. Bellah (eds.), *Religion in America* (Boston: Beacon Press, 1968), 282.

10. Joseph L. Blau, "Alternatives Within Contemporary American Judaism," ibid., 299-311.

11. John Courtney Murray, *We Hold These Truths* (New York: Sheed & Ward, 1960), 50, 54. This position has been ably argued by others, most notably Robert F. Drinan, *Religion, the Courts and Public Policy* (New York: McGraw-Hill, 1963). Several Justices have worried lest some Supreme Court decisions be interpreted as manifestations of hostility toward religion, and have gone out of their way to deny it. See text for notes 54-58 and 67-68 *infra*.

12. Mead, *Lively Experiment*, 66.

13. Alexis de Tocqueville, *Democracy in America*, 289.

14. See Justice Burger's statement that "political division along religious lines was one of the principal evils against which the First Amendment was intended to protect." *Lemon* v. *Kurtzman*, 402 U.S. 602, 622 (1971). The reference is to Paul Freund, "Aid to Parochial Schools," *Harvard Law Review* 82 (1969): 1692.

15. See Murray, *op. cit.*, 63-69.

16. Padover, *op. cit.*, 519.

17. Letter of 1832 to Rev. Jasper Adams, in Gaillard Hunt (ed.),

The Writings of James Madison, vol. 9 (New York: G.P. Putnam's Sons, 1904), 487. Madison noted that "it may not be easy, in every possible case, to trace the line of separation. . . ."

18. See the thoughtful analysis by Sidney E. Mead, "Neither Church nor State: Reflections on James Madison's 'Line of Separation,' " *Journal of Church and State* 10 (1968): 349–63.

19. *Reynolds* v. *United States*, 93 U.S. 145, 164, (1878), affirmed the conviction of a Mormon resident of the Territory of Utah under a federal law making bigamy a crime in the territories. Jefferson had said that the powers of government could reach only the actions of men, not their opinions. Since polygamy was an action, the government could therefore deny its enjoyment, even though Reynolds alleged that he was ordered by his church to practice it.

20. *Everson* v. *Board of Education*, 330 U.S. 1, 16 (1947).

21. Charles Reich, "Mr. Justice Black," *Harvard Law Review* 76 (1963): 736. Note also Justice Jackson's puzzled remark in his *Everson* dissent: "The undertones of the opinion, advocating complete and uncompromising separation . . . seem utterly discordant with its conclusion." (330 U.S. at 19)

22. *McCollum* v. *Board of Education*, 333 U.S. 203, 247 (1948) (Reed, J. dissenting).

23. *Engel* v. *Vitale*, 370 U.S. 421, 445-46 (1962) (Stewart, J., dissenting).

24. *Zorach* v. *Clauson*, 343, U.S. 306, 325 (1952) (Jackson, J., dissenting).

25. *Wolman* v. *Walter*, 433 U.S. 229, 266 (1977) (Stevens, J., concurring in part and dissenting in part).

26. *Zorach* v. *Clauson*, 343 U.S. at 312.

27. *Abington School District* v. *Schempp*, 374 U.S. 203, 231, 294 (1963) (Brennan, J., concurring).

28. *Board of Education* v. *Allen* 392 U.S. 236, 242 (1968).

29. *Walz* v. *Tax Commission*, 397 U.S. 664, 669-70 (1970). Dissenting in this case, Justice Douglas said: "There is a line between what a State may do in encouraging 'religious' activities . . . and what a State may not do by using its resources to promote 'religious' activities . . . or bestowing benefits because of them. Yet that line may not always be clear." Ibid., at 701.

30. *Lemon* v. *Kurtzman*, 403 U.S. at 612.

31. *Braunfeld* v. *Brown*, 366 U.S. 599 (1961).

32. *Sherbert* v. *Verner*, 374 U.S. 398 (1963). This same strict scrutiny test was applied by Chief Justice Burger in ruling against a New Hampshire law prohibiting Jehovah's Witnesses from obscuring the state motto on their car license plate because they found it repugnant to their religious belief. *Wooley* v. *Maynard*, 430 U.S. 705 (1977). But Justice

White (a dissenter in *Sherbert*) refused to apply the high *Sherbert* standard for government to a private employer under Title VII of the 1964 Civil Rights Act prohibiting religious discrimination. TWA, the employer, had fired an employee for a refusal to work on Saturday, yet was not required to deprive senior employees of their seniority rights (regarding work on Saturday) in order to accommodate a junior employee's religious practices. The duty to accommodate, said White, did not require TWA to take steps inconsistent with an otherwise valid union agreement. *Trans World Airlines, Inc.* v. *Hardison*, 432 U.S. 63 (1977). Justice Marshall in dissent correctly saw this holding as a limitation on *Sherbert*.

Another limitation on *Sherbert* was the 1985 decision declaring unconstitutional a Connecticut statute that gave employees an unqualified right not to work on their chosen Sabbath. The Court held 8-1 that it was a violation of the Establishment Clause for Connecticut to place an absolute obligation on religious practices of employees, because this had the effect of giving Sabbath religious concerns automatic control over all secular interests at the workplace. The Court expressly noted that there was no exception in the Connecticut law allowing for an employer's substantial economic burdens, such as existed in the more flexible statutes on Sabbath observance in at least thirty other states. Accommodation for religious freedom, therefore, could not mean that in every situation an employer can be compelled to act in the name of religion. *Estate of Thornton* v. *Caldor, Inc.*, 105 S.Ct. 2914 (1985).

33. *Wisconsin* v. *Yoder*, 406 U.S. 205, 216 (1972). See the helpful discussion by William C. Shepherd, *To Serve the Blessings of Liberty — American Constitutional Law and the New Religious Movements* (New York: Crossroad, 1985), 7-37.

34. *Abington School District* v. *Schempp*, 374 U.S. at 312 (Stewart, J., dissenting). Justice Stewart's position, first elaborated in his *Engel* dissent (*supra* note 23), is narrower than this statement would indicate. He holds that if there is no coercion of the individual conscience by imposition of some belief or practice, then there can be no establishment problem, since that clause forbids only an official state church.

35. *Davis* v. *Beason*, 133 U.S. 333, 342 (1890).

36. *United States* v. *Macintosh*, 283 U.S. 605, 623 (1931) (Hughes, C. J., dissenting).

37. *United States* v. *Ballard*, 322 U.S. 78, 86-87 (1944). The case involved the prosecution for fraud of the founder of the "I Am" sect for telling his followers that his wife had shaken hands with Jesus, that he had been selected as divine messenger and had the divine power of healing incurable diseases. Justice Jackson's dissent concluded that "the price of freedom of religion . . . is that we must put up with, and even pay for, a good deal of rubbish," but that such beliefs "ought not be the subject of judicial examination." Ibid., at 95.

38. *Torcaso* v. *Watkins*, 367 U.S. 488, 495 n. 11 (1961).

39. *United States* v. *Seeger*, 380 U.S. 163, 184-85 (1965).

40. *Welsh* v. *United States*, 398 U.S. 333, 342, (1970).

41. This and other justifications for *Welsh's* definition of religion are discussed at length by John Paris, "Toward an Understanding of the Supreme Court's approach to Religion in Conscientious Objector Cases," *Suffolk University Law Review* 7 (1973): 449.

42. *Gillette* v. *United States*, 401 U.S. 437, 454 (1971). Justice Marshall wrote for the court in this case of a conscientious objection, not to all wars, but only to "unjust" wars such as that in Vietnam. He interpreted §6 (j) as having but one meaning: "that conscientious scruples relating to war and military service must amount to conscientious opposition to participating personally in any and all war." Ibid., at 443. Congress' decision to exempt in this way admittedly worked a discriminatory effect via-à-vis the religious beliefs of different claimants, but this discrimination was not an establishment of religion, because the reasons for so limiting the exemption were not religious but secular and neutral. Moreover, these substantial government reasons (an interest in the fairness of administrative decision-making and in the necessity of procuring manpower necessary for military purposes) were strong enough to justify the impact upon the free exercise claim of conscientious objectors to particular wars.

43. *Abington School District* v. *Schempp*, 374 U.S. at 245-46 (Brennan, J., concurring).

44. *Supra* note 20.

45. *McCollum* v. *Board of Education*, *supra* note 22.

46. *Zorach* v. *Clauson*, *supra* note 24.

47. *Abington School District* v. *Schempp*, 374 U.S. at 217, 222.

48. *Board of Education* v. *Allen*, *supra* note 28.

49. *Walz* v. *Tax Commission*, *supra* note 29.

50. *Tilton* v. *Richardson*, 403 U.S. 672 (1971). Higher education also survived the three tests in *Hunt* v. *McNair*, 413 U.S. 734 (1973), and *Roemer* v. *Maryland*, 426 U.S. 736 (1976).

51. *Lemon* v. *Kurtzman*, *supra* note 14.

52. *Committee for Public Education* v. *Nyquist*, 413 U.S. 756 (1973).

53. *Wolman* v. *Walter*, *supra* note 25.

54. *Mueller* v. *Allen*, 463 U.S. 388, 398-99, 395, 400 (1983). Rehnquist was joined by Burger, White, Powell, and O'Connor. Burger, White, and Rehnquist had dissented in *Nyquist*, the New York case, an opinion authored by Powell. In the present case, Marshall's dissent found that deductions for public school expenses were minor, and that 95 percent of private school students in Minnesota attended sectarian schools; hence the deductions in the Minnesota statute were really indistinguishable from the tuition grants and tax credits in the New York statute, and therefore both statutes were violations of the Establishment Clause.

55. *Zorach* v. *Clauson*, 343 U.S. at 313-14.

56. *Engel* v. *Vitale*, 370 U.S. at 434-35. In this case Douglas agreed with Black that it would not be neutral to permit the use of a "nondenominational" prayer prepared by the New York Board of Regents for use in public schools.

57. *Abington School District* v. *Schempp*, 374, U.S. at 225.

58. Ibid., at 256, 295 (Brennan J., concurring).

59. *Lemon* v. *Kurtzman*, 403 U.S. at 615.

60. *Marsh* v. *Chambers*, 463 U.S. 783, 786, 792, 788 (1983).

61. *Wallace* v. *Jaffree*, 105 S.Ct. 2479, 2492, 2491 (1985).

62. Philip B. Kurland, "Religion and the Law: of Church and State and Supreme Court," *The University of Chicago Law Review* 29 (1961):1.

63. *Walz* v. *Tax Commission*, 397 U.S. at 694. In the Welsh case (*supra* note 40) Harlan would have found the §6 (j) exemption for conscientious objectors to be unconstitutional, because it made this exemption only for "religious" objectors. Once Congress chose to exempt, it could not constitutionally draw the line between the exempt and non-exempt solely on religious grounds. Black's majority opinion, as we saw, simply expanded the meaning of "religion" to include everyone Harlan wished to see included. Hence his concurrence in the Welsh judgment. Needless to say, Harlan's strict neutrality was neither indifferent nor hostile to religion. He simply demanded that a classification which benefited religion should not do so *qua* religion, but on some other basis (e.g. tax exemption for churches as cultural or charitable institutions).

64. *Supra* note 29.

65. See text for notes 47 and 32 *supra*. Both Justices also use the word "strict" but not in the sense of Harland and Kurland.

66. "For the men who wrote the Religion Clauses of the First Amendment the 'establishment' of a religion connoted sponsorship, financial support, and active involvement of the sovereign in religious activity." *Walz* v. *Tax Commission*, 397 U.S. at 669.

67. Ibid., at 668-69. Two cases illustrate how these two clauses sometimes overlap. The first is the Court's 1981 decision, *Widmar* v. *Vincent*. The University of Missouri at Kansas City routinely permitted over a hundred official student groups to use its facilities for meetings, but refused to allow religious groups to use space for worship. The University's prohibition was based on the Establishment Clause, but Justice Powell, writing for a majority of eight, focused upon the free exercise and equal access rights of the religious groups. Having created a forum generally open to student groups, he said, the University could not use a content-based exclusion of religious speech, since state regulation of speech must be content-neutral. Nor was there an establishment barrier. Equal access for religious groups would not have the primary effect of advancing religion, because "an

open forum in a public university does not confer any imprimatur of state approval on religious sects or practices," but rather furthers "the neutral purpose of developing students' social and cultural awareness as well as their intellectual curiosity." Moreover, there would be a greater risk of entanglement in a policy requiring the University to monitor which forms of speech are worship and which are not. 454 U.S. 263, 274, 267.

The second case is *National Labor Relations Board* v. *Catholic Bishop of Chicago*, which decided in 1979 that the N.L.R.B. had no jurisdiction over lay teachers in religious schools because Congress did not intend the National Labor Relations Act to apply to church-operated schools. The U.S. Court of Appeals for the Seventh Circuit had declared the Act unconstitutional as applied to parochial schools, because any Board action would impinge on the freedom of church authorities to shape and direct teaching, and would thus have a chilling effect on religious freedom. What is interesting is that the 5 to 4 majority opinion not only avoided any constitutional question, but did not even mention free exercise of religion; instead it emphasized entanglement, an Establishment Clause doctrine, as the potential constitutional violation arising from compulsory collective bargaining. See 440 U.S. 490.

68. See Paul Kauper, "The *Walz* Decision: More on the Religious Clauses of the First Amendment," *Michigan Law Review* 69 (1970):179.

69. See Mark DeWolfe Howe, *The Garden and the Wilderness* (Chicago: University of Chicago Press, 1965); Wilbur Katz, "Freedom of Religion and State Neutrality," *The University of Chicago Law Review* 20 (1953):426; Edward S. Corwin, "The Supreme Court as National School Board," *Law and Contemporary Problems* 14 (1949):3; Erwin N. Griswold, "Absolute is in the Dark," *Utah Law Review* 8 (1963):167. Their opinions are discussed at length by Richard E. Morgan, *The Supreme Court and Religion* (New York: The Free Press, 1972), 183ff.

70. *Sherbert* v. *Verner*, 374 U.S. at 422 (Harlan, J., dissenting).

71. *Abington School District* v. *Schempp*, 374 U.S. at 306 (Goldberg, J., concurring).

72. In his concurring opinion in *Walz*, Justice Brennan observed that Madison did not oppose Virginia's exemption of the churches, and that Jefferson was President when tax exemption was first given to Washington churches. See 397 U.S. at 684-85.

73. See text for notes 49-51 *supra*.

74. 397 U.S. at 672-78.

75. Ibid., at 675.

76. Ibid., at 674.

77. The court in *Walz* mentions only the charitable services of churches. But by far the most important service a church performs in society is to help its adherents to "make sense" of life, and par-

ticularly of those aspects of it which are both unsatisfactory and un-
alterable: failure, handicap, defeat, loss, illness, bereavement, and
the prospect of their own death. Explanations of these experiences
may be theistic or non-theistic, naturalistic or super-naturalistic, activist or quietist, conventional or bizarre. Not all citizens feel an equal
need at all times for such explanations of ultimate meaning, but the
fact that all religions provide them in one or other form has always
been thought to be important for the survival of society and for the
collective well-being of its members.

78. 397 U.S. at 673.

79. Boris I. Bittker and George K. Rahdert have argued persua-
sively that exemption of nonprofit organizations ought not to be
thought of as privilege any more than as a subsidy. For what is taxed
by the federal government is "net income," inuring in measurable
amounts to the direct or indirect personal benefit of identifiable natural
persons. By definition nonprofit organizations fall outside this category. It is impossible not to exempt them, since they are not within
the ambit of the concept which has been chosen to separate taxpayers
from non-taxpayers. See these authors' lengthy treatment of the subject in "The Exemption of Nonprofit Organizations from Federal Taxation," *Yale Law Journal* 85 (1976):299. See also Bittker's earlier article,
"Churches, Taxes and the Constitution," *Yale Law Journal* 78 (1969):
1285. Congress' decision in 1969 to impose a tax on the "unrelated
business income" of tax-exempt organizations, including churches,
is consistent with Bittker's analysis.

80. *Bob Jones University* v. *U.S.*, 461 U.S. 574, 591-92 (1983). The
suit arose because of an Internal Revenue Service decision in 1970
that to be exempt under Section 501(c)(3) an organization would have
to fall under the common law understanding of a charity in that it
would not contravene public policy. Burger argued that the inaction
of Congress since 1970 should be interpreted as support for the policy,
especially since members had repeatedly debated the ruling. In his
concurring opinion, Justice Powell said he was "unconvinced that the
critical question in determining tax-exempt status is whether an individual organization provides a clear 'public benefit' as defined by
the Court." He added: "Far from representing an effort to reinforce
any perceived 'common community conscience,' the provision of tax
exemptions to nonprofit groups is one indispensable means of limiting
the influence of governmental orthodoxy on important areas of community life." While Powell was convinced that the need for uniformity in racial discrimination policies was strong enough for him to
side with the majority in this case, he worried about other cases in
which the tolerance and encouragement of diversity might be desirable, or at least permissible. Ibid., at 608-09.

81. *Lynch* v. *Donnelly*, 104 S.Ct. 1355. 1359-62 (1984). The Chief

Justice was joined by Justices White, Powell, Rehnquist, and O'Connor.

82. Ibid., at 1365-66. The dissenting opinion, written by Justice Brennan and joined by Justices Marshall, Blackmun, and Stevens, pointed out that it was not clear whether the Court would have upheld a display that consisted solely of a crèche, or of another religious symbol, such as a cross. "But the City's action," said Brennan, should be recognized as "a coercive, though perhaps small, step toward establishing the sectarian preference of the majority at the expense of the minority." Ibid., at 1386.

83. *Abington School District* v. *Schempp*, 374 U.S. at 222.

84. Ibid., at 226, note 10. Justice Brennan makes the same point in his concurrence. Ibid., at 299.

85. Obviously this freedom is not unlimited, as the courts have decided when dealing with questions like polygamy, snake handling, etc. The juridical criterion for such limitation is the extent to which a particular form of religious expression seriously violates either the public peace, or commonly accepted standards of public morality, or the rights of other citizens. For examples of the latter limitation see cases cited in note 32 *supra*.

86. See the study of the French system by Robert M. Healey, *The French Achievement: Private School Aid* (New York: Paulist Press, 1974).

87. See the authors mentioned in note 69 *supra*.

88. See text for notes 49-51 *supra*.

89. *Supra* note 28.

90. *Lemon* v. *Kurtzman*, 403 U.S. at 665 (White, J., dissenting).

91. Ibid., at 668.

92. Ibid., at 640 (Douglas, J., concurring). Italics added.

93. Ibid., at 622-23. See note 14 *supra*.

94. *Tilton* v. *Richardson*, 403 U.S. at 688. Presumably this is also the ultimate reason that churches were supported in *Walz*; whatever else may be said, tax exemption is an ongoing, low visibility governmental practice, lacking the divisive potential of new grant programs, which must be legislated for in controversy, and then very visibly funded and administered.

95. In *Meek* v. *Pittinger*, four years after *Lemon*, Justice Brennan chided the plurality for not acknowledging this test more openly, and for not explicitly giving to it the weight which in fact it carries in the Court's decision-making. 421 U.S. 349, 374 (1975). Brennan was joined by Justices Marshall and Douglas. Between *Lemon* and *Meek* the test was mentioned once in *Committee for Public Education* v. *Nyquist*, 413 U.S. at 795-96.

96. *Grand Rapids School District* v. *Ball*, 105 S.Ct. 3216, 3223, 3224, 3225, 3230 (1985). Grand Rapids also had a Community Education program in which full-time *parochial* school teachers were paid to teach secular subjects after regular school hours under *parochial* school super-

vision. Chief Justice Burger and Justice O'Connor joined the majority in ruling 7-2 against its constitutionality.

97. *Aguilar* v. *Felton*, 105 S.Ct. 3232, 3239, 3243, 3248 (1985).

98. Feature story in *The New York Times* for August 25, 1985.

99. Freund, *art. cit.*, 1692. Jesse Choper has asked a question which neither Freund nor the Court nor anyone else has answered, and for which there may be no answer. Why, he asks, is it so easily assumed that the no-support rule here will eventually result in less political strife than some effort to allocate fairly? With Catholic schools financially pressed on every side and forced in many cases to close, is it not possible that a no-aid policy will in the end be productive of more political conflict than a policy of equal-aid? See "The Establishment Clause and Aid to Parochial Schools," *California Law Review* 56 (1968): 260.

100. Morgan, *op. cit.*, 202.

Chapter 3

1. See the excellent contemporary study of morality in public life by Francis X. Winters, *Politics and Ethics* (New York: Paulist Press, 1975).

2. John Courtney Murray comments on these contrasts between law and morality in *We Hold These Truths* (New York: Sheed and Ward, 1960), 160-65.

3. Ibid., 166-67.

4. See the perceptive article of Ralph C. Chandler, "Ethics and Public Policy," *Commonweal*, May 12, 1978.

5. Grant Gilmore, *The Ages of American Law* (New Haven: Yale University Press, 1976), 160.

6. See Winters, *op. cit.*, 18-19, 47-48.

7. On public happiness, see Hannah Arendt, *On Revolution* (New York: Viking Press, 1965), 123 ff; Christopher F. Mooney, *Religion and the American Dream*, 44ff.

8. The astute collection of essays by George F. Will, *The Pursuit of Happiness and Other Sobering Thoughts* (New York: Harper and Row, 1979), would dispute this understanding of public happiness. Will would agree much more with Alexander Hamilton than with Madison that true public interest can be realized only through the decisions of a disinterested elite who alone can define, achieve, and protect what is valuable in life and history, and who know antecedently to any public discussion what is genuinely important and excellent and what is not.

9. H. L. A. Hart, *The Concept of Law* (New York: Oxford University Press, 1961), 48.

10. Duncan MacRae, Jr., discusses professions as sources of public values in *The Social Function of Social Science* (New Haven: Yale University Press, 1976), 25-28.

11. Cited by Donald R. Cressey, "White Collar Subversives," *The Center Magazine*, November/December, 1978, 46-47.

12. See on this point, Geoffrey C. Hazard, Jr., *Ethics in the Practice of Law* (New Haven: Yale University Press, 1978), xii-xiii.

13. Ibid., xiv.

14. Geoffrey C. Hazard, Jr., "Capitalist Ethics," *Yale Alumni Magazine*, April 1978, 50-51.

15. Quoted in *Time*, June 19, 1978, 33.

16. See the perceptive treatment of Solzhenitsyn's speech by John Garvey, "In Defense of Solzhenitsyn," *Commonweal*, September 1, 1978.

17. Daniel J. Boorstin, *Time*, June 19, 1978, 21.

18. Garvey, *op. cit.*, pursues this point at some length.

19. In his latest work, *Statecraft as Soulcraft* (New York: Simon and Schuster, 1983), George F. Will continues to be concerned that this approach of Madison will atomize American society instead of fostering stable communities with a sense of common purpose and shared spiritual tradition. He argues that the role of government decisions in such an enterprise is actively to initiate and to extend the law's expression of morality and duty as far as is reasonable and in as wide a sweep as prudence allows. There is no need for government to wait until the democratic processes have grappled with all the moral choices and worked through all the moral conflicts. His suspicion of these processes and the minimal moral choices they produce appears in his assertion that "the basic political right is to good government, not self-government."

20. See John Murray Cuddihy, *No Offense: Civil Religion and Protestant Taste.*

21. Alfred North Whitehead, *Science and the Modern World* (Cambridge: Cambridge University Press, 1927), 245.

22. These are the emphases of Larry R. Churchill, "The Professionalization of Ethics," *Soundings* 60 (1977): 41-44.

23. For more on this cooperation, see James F. Bresnahan and John L. Kane, "Professional Ethics and Competence in Trial Practice," *American Bar Association Journal*, April 1976, 989-91.

24. Monroe H. Freedman, *Lawyers' Ethics in an Adversary System* (Indianapolis: Bobbs Merrill, 1975).

25. David E. Price has explored some of these underlying assumptions of the adversary system in "Law and Liberalism: The Adversary System in Context," *Soundings* 60 (1977): 72-87.

26. John Henry Newman, *The Idea of a University*, Lecture V (Notre Dame: University of Notre Dame Press edition, 1982), 91.

Chapter 4

1. See Warren E. Burger, "The State of Justice," *American Bar Association Journal*, April 1984, 62-66; see also the lengthy article by Stuart Taylor, Jr., on page one of *The New York Times* for June 1, 1983, dealing with the judicial system.

2. Everett C. Hughes, "Professions," *Daedalus* 92 (1963): 657. See also Bernard Barber, "Some Problems in the Sociology of the Professions," Ibid., 669-88; Duncan MacRae, Jr., "Professions and Social Sciences as Sources of Public Values," *Soundings* 60 (1977): 3-21.

3. Lois G. Forer, "Some Problems in the Administration of Justice in a Secularized Society," *Mercer Law Review* 31 (1980): 449.

4. Jerold S. Auerbach, "A Plague of Lawyers," *Harper's*, October 1976, 38.

5. See the discussion of these issues by Thomas L. Shaffer, *On Being a Christian and a Lawyer* (Provo: Brigham Young University Press, 1981), 160-64; Jerold S. Auerbach, *Justice Without Law?* (New York: Oxford University Press, 1983), 138-47.

6. John T. Noonan, Jr., *Persons and Masks of the Law* (New York: Farrar, Straus and Giroux, 1976), xii. The quotation is from *De moribus ecclesiae catholicae et de moribus Manichaeorum* in J. P. Migne, ed., *Patrologia latina*, vol. 32, 1322.

7. Noonan, *op. cit.*, 18.

8. Harold J. Berman, "The Influence of Christianity Upon the Development of Law," *Oklahoma Law Review* 12 (1959): 88.

9. Shaffer, *op. cit.* 162.

10. Alexis de Tocqueville, *Democracy in America*, 270.

11. Lawrence M. Friedman, *A History of American Law* (New York: Simon and Schuster, 1975), 20-21.

12. Maxwell Bloomfield, *American Lawyers in a Changing Society, 1776-1876* (Cambridge: Harvard University Press, 1976), 54.

13. Jethro K. Lieberman, *The Litigious Society* (New York: Basic Books, 1983), 15.

14. Harold J. Berman, "The Interaction of Law and Religion," *Mercer Law Review* 31 (1980): 412.

15. Ibid., 409.

16. John Naisbitt, "Megatrends for Lawyers and Clients," *American Bar Association Journal*, June 1984, 45-46.

17. As reported in *The New York Times*, July 9, 1984.

18. Auerbach, *op.cit.*, 121.

19. Douglas Sturm, "American Legal Realism and the Covenantal Myth: World Views in the Practice of Law," *Mercer Law Review* 31 (1980): 488. Sturm's article is a masterly analysis of our legal profession's reigning jurisprudence.

20. Karl N. Llewellyn, "Some Realism About Realism," *Harvard*

Law Review 44 (1931): 1237; Jerome Frank, *Law and the Modern Mind* (New York: Doubleday & Company, 1963), 112. For an overview of the movement, see Lon Fuller, "American Legal Philosophy at Mid-Century," *Journal of Legal Education* 6 (1954): 457-85.

21. Oliver Wendell Holmes, Jr., "The Path of the Law," *Harvard Law Review* 10 (1897): 461.

22. Oliver Wendell Holmes, Jr., *The Common Law* (Cambridge: Harvard University Press edition, 1963), 5.

23. Sturm, *art. cit.*, 495.

24. Holmes, *The Common Law*, 38, 36.

25. Karl N. Llewellyn, *Jurisprudence: Realism in Theory and Practice* (Chicago: University of Chicago Press, 1962), 36. Quoted by Sturm, *art. cit.*, 496.

26. Hans Kelsen, *The General Theory of Law* (New York: Russell & Russell, 1945), 5.

27. Quoted in Harold J. Berman, "Philosophical Aspects of American Law," in *Talks on American Law*, ed. Harold J. Berman (New York: Vintage Books, 1961), 229.

28. Llewellyn, *Jurisprudence*, 86. Quoted by Sturm, *art. cit.*, 497.

29. Karl N. Llewellyn, *The Bramble Bush* (Dobbs Ferry: Oceana Publications, 1960), 12. Italics in original.

30. Karl N. Llewellyn, paraphrased by Lon Fuller, "American Legal Realism," *University of Pennsylvania Law Review* 82 (1934): 439.

31. Leiberman, *op. cit.*, 169.

32. John H. Wigmore, *Evidence in Trials in Common Law*, vol. 3 (Boston: Little, Brown and Company, 1923), 1367. Quoted by Lieberman, *op. cit.*, 168.

33. See, for example, Anne Strick, *Injustice For All* (New York: G.P. Putnam's Sons, 1977); Marvin E. Frankel, *Partisan Justice* (New York: Hill and Wang, 1980); Jerold S. Auerbach, *Unequal Justice: Lawyers and Social Change in Modern America* (New York: Oxford University Press, 1976).

34. From the preface of Langdell's 1871, *Cases on the Law of Contracts*, quoted by Robert S. Redmont, "Legal Education: The Beat of a Different Drummer," *New York University Law Review* 53 (1978): 677.

35. Grant Gilmore, *The Ages of American Law* (New Haven: Yale University Press, 1977), 47.

36. Ibid., 54. Gilmore's critique of this hypothesis is severe, and his judgment of Holmes as a person no less so. Far from being the tolerant aristocrat and defender of liberties as the myth would have it, the "real Holmes was savage, harsh and cruel, a bitter and lifelong pessimist who saw in the course of human life nothing but a continuing struggle in which the rich and powerful impose their will on the poor and weak." Ibid., 49.

37. Ibid., 46-47.

38. Noonan, *op. cit.*, 6.
39. Gilmore, *op. cit.*, 87.
40. Elizabeth Dvorkin, Jack Himmelstein, and Howard Lesnick, *Becoming a Lawyer* (St. Paul: West Publishing Company, 1981), 1.
41. Redmont, *art. cit.*, 685.
42. Alfred North Whitehead, *Science and the Modern World* (Cambridge: Cambridge University Press, 1927), 245.
43. Llewellyn, *The Bramble Bush*, 101. A new movement in American legal education, known as "critical legal theory," is a more radical form of legal realism and takes as its starting point that the analytic reasoning learned in law schools cannot of itself provide either a method or a process for answering particular legal questions or for leading reasonable people to particular results in particular cases. Rather what accomplishes this are the very political, social, moral, and religious value judgments from which most lawyers and judges claim to be independent. This does not mean that rule, principle, and policy analysis become unimportant, or that all outcomes in a given case are equally likely, but simply that any particular outcome is determined chiefly by its social context. That is to say, in a specific context one legal rationale among many will seem to be more reasonable or more "right" than the others because the values of that particular context support that result. Unlike legal realists, however, critical legal theorists do not deal with the instrumentality of law but with its legitimacy. They deny that law is a constraint on power or a protection against it; rather it is part of a structure of power favoring the rich over the poor and always legitimating the status quo. Very important consequences would obviously follow from "critical legal theory," for legal education, the courts, and for the legal profession generally. But while the number of its adherents is growing, the extent of its influence as well as its broader objectives for the restructuring of society are still not clear. Apparently very important differences of opinion exist among those who consider themselves critical theorists. See the collection of essays by the leading theorists edited by David Kairys, *The Politics of Law* (New York: Pantheon, 1982), especially the essay by Harvard Professor Duncan Kennedy, "Legal Education as Training for Hierarchy," pp. 40-61.
44. See *The Chronicle of Higher Education*, January 18, 1984, for a full report on this unusual meeting.
45. Derek C. Bok, "A Flawed System," *Harvard Magazine*, May/June 1983, 45, 39-40.
46. Auerbach, *Justice Without Law?*, 142.
47. Bok, *art. cit.*, 41.
48. Quoted by Errol G. Rohr, "An Interaction: Theology and Legal Education," *Capital University Law Review* 8 (1979): 436.
49. Quoted in *The New York Times*, April 30, 1984.

50. Scott Turrow, *One L* (New York: Putnam, 1977), 100.

51. Ibid., 147, note 15.

52. Quoted in *The New York Times*, June 1, 1983.

53. Peter Megargee Brown, "Misguided Lawyers," *The New York Times*, December 6, 1983. See also Tamar Lewin, "The New National Law Firms," *The New York Times*, October 4, 1984.

54. Bok, *art. cit.*, 42.

55. Ibid., 45.

56. Marvin E. Frankel, "An Immodest Proposal," *The New York Times Magazine*, December 4, 1977, 96.

57. See the development of this argument by Monroe Freedman, *Lawyers' Ethics in an Adversary System* (Indianapolis: Bobbs-Merrill, 1975).

58. Quoted by Philip M. Stern, "Lawyers and Ethics," *The New York Times*, August 4, 1980.

59. This dilemma is discussed at length by Charles Fried, "The Lawyer as Friend: The Moral Foundations of the Lawyer-Client Relation," *Yale Law Journal* 85 (1976): 1060ff.

60. See James F. Bresnahan, "Ethics and the Study and Practice of Law," *Journal of Legal Education* 28 (1976): 189ff.

61. Richard Wasserstrom, "Lawyers as Professionals: Some Moral Issues," *Human Rights* 5 (1975): 5, 8.

62. Quoted in *The New York Times*, June 1, 1983.

63. Bok, *art. cit*, 44-45.

64. Quoted in Susan K. Boyd, "A Look at Legal Education in the 21st Century," *Syllabus* 15 (1984): 1, 4, 8.

65. Grant Gilmore, "What is a Law School?" *Connecticut Law Review* 15 (1982), 3.

66. Charles L. Black, *Law as an Art* (Knoxville: University of Tennessee Press, 1978), 14.

67. Noonan, *op. cit.*, 17.

68. Wasserstrom, *art. cit.*, 15-23.

69. Shaffer, *op. cit.*, 22, 29.

70. Ibid., 30.

71. Burger, *art. cit.*, 66.

72. On this approach see Shaffer, *op. cit.*, 87-92, 135-39.

73. Multiple examples of such power are given in a study cited earlier by Jerold Auerbach, *Unequal Justice*, and in Mark Green, *The Other Government: The Unseen Power of Washington Lawyers* (New York: Grossman Publishers, 1975).

74. Paul A. Freund, "The Legal Profession," *Daedalus* 92 (1963): 690-92.

75. Lawrence M. Friedman, *American Law* (New York: W. W. Norton & Company, 1984).

76. See Douglas Sturm, "Modernity and the Meaning of Law,"

Worldview, September 1979, 48-51.

77. Quoted in Boyd, *art. cit.*, 4. I do not wish to become involved here in the very important but seemingly endless current discussion of the lawyer-client relationship within the narrow context of the Code of Professional Responsibility and the Model Rules of Professional Conduct. To do so would force us to deal in great detail with highly specialized subject matter. Whether these rules are to be understood as ethical or legal norms is one unresolved issue. Another is the interpretation of "zealous advocacy," and the relation of the "hired gun" interpretation of such advocacy to the interpretation suggested by the Cramton quotation. For examples of different points of view in this intra-professional debate and the dilemmas posed by certain lawyer-client situations, see Norman Redlich, *Professional Responsibility* (Boston: Little, Brown and Company, 1983); Geoffrey C. Hazard, Jr., *Ethics in the Practice of Law;* Monroe Freedman, *op. cit.*

78. The Legal Services Corporation has become a focus of controversy for several reasons. Critics perceive the program as a political instrument of activist lawyers that is inefficient both in helping the poor and in the cost it places on the legal system. Defenders insist that there is every reason to make a large and fallible government accountable in its own courts for violating the legal rights of the poor. A dispassionate assessment of these and other underlying issues is given by Roger C. Cramton, "Why Legal Services for the Poor?" *American Bar Association Journal,* May 1982, 550-56.

79. See on this value question the comments of Edward M. Gaffney, Jr., in "Biblical Religion and Constitutional Adjudication in a Secularized Society," *Mercer Law Review* 31 (1980): 422-48.

80. For this insight I am indebted to Harold J. Berman, "The influence of Christianity. . . ," 88-89.

81. Black, *op. cit.*, 13.

82. Benjamin N. Cardozo, *The Nature of the Judicial Process* (New Haven: Yale University Press, 1971), 166.

83. Quoted by Frederick M. Rowe, "For Grant Gilmore: A Student's Lament," *Yale Law Report* 29 (1982): 11.

Chapter 5

1. Edwin Borchard and William Potter Lage, *Neutrality for the United States,* 2nd ed. (New Haven: Yale University Press, 1940), 144.

2. Colin Simpson, *The Lusitania* (New York: Ballantine Books, 1974).

3. Harley Notter, *The Origins of the Foreign Policy of Woodrow Wilson* (Baltimore: The Johns Hopkins Press, 1937), 373. My other sources for Wilson's views and motives are Arthur S. Link, *Wilson: The Struggle*

For Neutrality 1914-1915 (Princeton: Princeton University Press, 1960), and Ray Stannard Baker, *Woodrow Wilson, Life and Letters, Neutrality 1914-1915* (New York: Doubleday, Doran & Company, 1935).

4. Link, *op. cit.*, 312-14.

5. *Papers Relating to the Foreign Relations of the United States, 1915 Supplement* (Washington: Government Printing Office, 1930), 95-97, Hereafter: *1915 Supplement*.

6. Ibid., 98-100. Link, *op. cit.*, 321-23.

7. *1915 Supplement*, 112-15.

8. *Papers Relating to the Foreign Relations of the United States, The Lansing Papers*, 1914-1920, vol. I (Washington: Government Printing Office, 1939), 373. Hereafter: *Lansing Papers*. Lengthy discussion of this complicated legal question will be found in Borchard and Lage, *op. cit.*, 83-124.

9. Ibid., 129.

10. Ibid., 94-100.

11. Link, *op. cit.*, 323-24. Simpson (*op. cit.*, 68-69) gives the impression that the whole question of Americans on belligerent ships was argued out before the "strict accountability" note was written, citing as evidence Lansing's use of Justice Marshall's opinion in the *Nereide* case. But Lansing's memorandum on this issue was not written until March 14, 1916. His prior mention of *Nereide* was in a ruling on September 19, 1914, which dealt with the very different issue of whether merchant vessels carrying arms for defense acquired the character of ships of war. Borchard and Lage (*op. cit.*, 127-128) argue from Wilson's later interpretation of "strict accountability" in the first *Lusitania* note that in his mind the phrase always referred to any violation of the cruiser rules resulting in an American death. But this is a presumption; the opposite is to be presumed from the evidence at this time. On the Lansing and the *Nereide* see ibid., 88-90; 117-22.

12. *Lansing Papers*, 375.

13. Borchard and Lage, *op. cit.*, 128-36.

14. On the Bryan-Lansing debate see Notter, *op. cit.*, 399-400; Baker, *op. cit.*, 265-73; Link, *op. cit.*, 359-63.

15. *Lansing Papers*, 378, Italics added.

16. Ibid., 369. See also Notter, *op. cit.*, 400-03.

17. Arthur S. Link, *Wilson the Diplomatist* (Baltimore: The Johns Hopkins Press, 1957), 13, 17, 21.

18. *1915 Supplement*, 419.

19. *Lansing Papers*, 420.

20. Ibid., 438.

21. Link, *Wilson*, 379-81. See also Baker, *op. cit.*, 331. His biographers agree that Wilson had a turbulent emotional makeup which he successfully concealed by keeping it under severe control. He once candidly admitted this to a meeting of the National Press Club: "If

I were to interpret myself, I would say that my constant embarrassment is to restrain the emotions that are inside me. You may not believe it, but I sometimes feel like a fire from a far from extinct volcano, and if the lava does not seem to spill over it is because you are not high enough to see into the basin and see the cauldron boil." Quoted in Earl Latham (ed.), *The Philosophy and Policies of Woodrow Wilson* (Chicago: University of Chicago Press, 1958), 11.

22. *Lansing Papers*, 386.

23. Simpson, *op. cit.*, 89; Baker, *op. cit.*, 324-25.

24. *Lansing Papers*, 387-88.

25. Ibid., 392, Italics added.

26. *1915 Supplement*, 394-39.

27. Quotations from the *Literary Digest*, May 22, 1915; Link, *Wilson*, 396; Baker *op. cit.*, 343.

28. *1915 Supplement*, 420.

29. *Lansing Papers*, 417-20.

30. Ibid., 429-544. Nevertheless, as Borchard and Lage point out (*op. cit.*, 157-58), the Report states that, after the bow and stern decks, Malone inspected the promenade deck, whereas, according to deck plans, six of the twelve guns would have been mounted one deck below, on the shelter deck. They still conclude that the ship did not carry guns.

31. *Lansing Papers*, 423-25.

32. Ibid., 428.

33. Ibid., 432. Italics added.

34. Ibid., 373. Italics added in the second part.

35. Ibid., 427.

36. Ibid., 450.

37. Simpson, *op. cit.*, 181-82, quoting unpublished material in Lansing's papers.

38. *Lansing Papers*, 418. See the text of the first note cited in note 26 *supra*.

39. See references in note 8 *supra*.

40. See texts cited in notes 24 and 25 *supra*.

41. *Lansing Papers*, 450.

42. Link, *Wilson*, 412.

43. *Lansing Papers*, 411, 421.

44. *1915 Supplement*, 437.

45. *Lansing Papers*, 439.

46. Link, *Wilson*, 431-55.

47. *Lansing Papers*, 451-52.

48. Simpson, *op. cit.*, 246.

49. Ibid., 225-28.

50. Borchard and Lage, *op. cit.*, 156.

51. Simpson, *op. cit.*, 94, 184-86.

52. *Lansing Papers*, 411, 438.
53. Notter, *op. cit.*, 219.

Chapter 6

1. Cicero *De Republica* 3.33; Sophocles, *Antigone* 450ff. See A.P. D'Entrèves, *Natural Law* (London: Hutchinson, 1970), and D. J. O'Connor, *Aquinas and Natural Law* (London: Macmillan, 1967).

2. Justinian *Digest* 1.1.1ff.

3. *Summa Theologica*, I-II, ques. 91, art. 2. See also art. 1.

4. Ibid., ques. 94, art. 2.

5. *In decem libros Ethicorum expositio* 1.3.38. See also *Summa Theologica*, I-II, ques. 94, art. 2 and 6. I have adopted here the insights of Columba Ryan, "The Traditional Concept of Natural Law: An Interpretation," in Illtud Evans (ed.), *Light on the Natural Law* (Baltimore: Helicon, 1965), 18-19, 27-31.

6. *Summa Theologica*, I-II, ques. 94, art. 4 and 6; *De Malo*, ques. 2, art. 4 and 13.

7. *Summa Theologica*, I-II, ques. 94, art. 5; Supplement, ques. 41, art. 1, ad. 3. Thomas' succinct principle, "diversa diversis mensuris mensurantur," appears in I-II, ques. 104, art. 3, ad 1. See Joseph Fuchs, *Natural Law* (New York: Sheed & Ward, 1965), 85-119.

8. Ryan, *op. cit.*, 34.

9. Louis Monden, *Sin, Liberty and Law* (New York: Sheed & Ward, 1965), 89.

10. See *Summa Theologica*, I-II, ques. 90, art. 1, ad 2; ques. 94, art. 1, ad 2.

11. As an example see John T. Noonan, Jr., *Contraception: A History of its Treatment by the Catholic Theologians and Canonists* (Cambridge: Harvard University Press, 1965), 57-106.

12. See the analysis of papal social teaching in David Hollenbach, *Claims in Conflict* (New York: Paulist Press, 1979), 107-33.

13. *Summa Theologica*, I-II, ques. 94, art. 4.

14. On these changes in outlook compare with earlier documents the following sections of *Gaudium et Spes*: §§10, 11, 22, 26, 41, 53 and 59. See also Hollenbach, *loc. cit.*

15. *Humanae Vitae*, §11, 12, 13, and 14.

16. The norm proposed in *Gaudium et Spes*, §51, is that the moral aspect of any procedure must be determined by objective standards "based on the nature of the human person and his acts." The church's response at various stages in the history of sexual morality is fascinating and has been traced by several scholars. For example, Noonan, *loc. cit.* and Margaret A. Farley, "Sexual Ethics," *Encyclopedia of Bioethics*, Vol. IV (New York: Free Press, 1978), 1575-89.

17. See *Humanae Vitae*, §10, 11, 13, 16, and 17. This shortcoming has been well addressed by J.A. Selling, "Moral Teaching, Traditional Teaching, and 'Humanae vitae,' " *Louvain Studies* 7 (1978): 24-44.

18. See Joseph A. Komonchak, "Humanae Vitae and Its Reception: Ecclesiological Reflections," *Theological Studies* 39 (1978): 250-57.

19. A special issue of *Chicago Studies* 17 (1978): 149-307, deals at length with these and similar questions.

Index